the
MIRACLE
MORNING

— UPDATED AND EXPANDED EDITION —

HAL ELROD

Real-Life Stories of Transformation
(from Miracle Morning Practitioners)

Read just a few to see what's possible for you . . .

"The Miracle Morning has changed my life completely. I HATED mornings, it was the worst part of the day for me. Then my sister told me about this book, and I knew it was my chance to change everything. So, I completed the 30-day challenge, and here I am: happy in the mornings, super-efficient, positive, and satisfied with nearly all aspects of my life."

—Jane Bavarova (3 years practicing the Miracle Morning)

"When my wife of 40 years died from cancer, I quit trying and gave up. I didn't have any hope or vision for the future. *The Miracle Morning* and the S.A.V.E.R.S. transformed me from feeling sorry for myself and living in the past to starting a new chapter in my life. Today is day number 255 of my Miracle Mornings, and I'm excited for today and tomorrow. So go for it. You can do it. And high five! You are a winner."

—Dan Copelin (10 months practicing the Miracle Morning)

"I am a mother of four boys and was feeling overwhelmed and like I wasn't living up to my potential. Then someone suggested I read *The Miracle Morning*, which I did, and I also watched the documentary. I was HOOKED! It has been an absolute game-changer. I'm so much more grateful for everything, I've started my own business, I'm about to publish a book, I'm so much more patient with my boys, and I even have them doing many of the S.A.V.E.R.S. themselves. I love my Miracle Mornings!"

—Jackie Emmett (2 years practicing the Miracle Morning)

"I've been doing the Miracle Morning for six months. I'm a father of two little guys, work full-time as an engineer, and have long been considered a night owl. After reading the book, I consciously decided to make a change, and now I get an extraordinary amount done each morning *before* everyone else wakes up. Making reading a priority every day has increased my knowledge greatly in a short amount of time, and scribing (journaling) enables me to consistently gain clarity and flesh out all my ideas in a constructive way. *The Miracle Morning* is a total mindset shift!"

—**Charlie Ussery (6 months practicing the Miracle Morning)**

"I'm on my sixtieth consecutive day of my Miracle Mornings. I have never done a habit for 60 days continuously, which in and of itself is an achievement. Here are just a few of the benefits:

1. My mind has been calmer than ever because of meditation/silence. I am being more conscious of my emotions.
2. My physical fitness has improved as I have cycled over 200 kilometers.
3. I am more organized in my daily activities and eliminate unnecessary tasks.
4. I am spending more time with family, and I have even inspired my wife and kids to do the Miracle Morning.

I am thankful to Hal for this wonderful book."

—**Dayananth Varun (2 months practicing the Miracle Morning)**

"I've been practicing the Miracle Morning for over seven years. It has been my guiding force through depression and anxiety, during infertility treatment, through the grief and loss of two of my triplets, and the extremely complex medical journey of my four-year-old. When people ask me how I've managed to keep a positive mindset throughout my devastating adversity over the last five years, my answer is always the same: *The Miracle Morning*. Without it, I'd be lost."

—Jessica Goodine (7 years practicing the Miracle Morning)

"The Miracle Morning has changed me at my core. I was never an early person or a consistent person. I would hit snooze 100 times. But with *The Miracle Morning* I found that I never wanted to miss a day because I was afraid I'd fall off the wagon. I know me, and I know that if I don't do it every day I won't continue. But I feel so accomplished, so productive, and so proud that I can say I've done this for over 150 days! I feel amazing every morning."

—Eleni Brooks (150 days practicing the Miracle Morning)

"I had accepted that I was not a morning person. After reading and implementing *The Miracle Morning*, I look forward to each morning now that I have one hour to myself. All my positive character traits are growing. I notice that I am more cheerful, energetic, alert, and so much more. I'm a better father, a better husband, a better friend, and a better colleague. I just started four weeks ago, and these are the benefits so far. I know I will grow so much more and take the lead over my own life instead of passively undergoing it."

—Bas Boska (30 days practicing the Miracle Morning)

"Before discovering *The Miracle Morning*, I was not a morning person. I remember reading the book and thinking about how I would love to feel inspired and motivated to live as the highest version of myself every day. At the time, I was inconsistent with my routines and habits, which often left me feeling frustrated and depleted. That all changed when I started doing S.A.V.E.R.S. Now, a year and a half later, I'm up at 5:15–5:30 AM every morning, including weekends! I strive for Level 10 living in four quadrants: Health, Wealth,

Self, and Others. It has been LIFE CHANGING!! I've lost 33 pounds, paid off two credit cards, and now seek to impact others each day with random acts of kindness. Blessing others is a true joy! I am so thankful I took a leap of faith and embraced the Miracle Morning and S.A.V.E.R.S. into my life!"

—Cathi Bingaman (18 months practicing the Miracle Morning)

Praise for *The Miracle Morning*

"*The Miracle Morning* is so much more than a book. It is a proven methodology that will help you fulfill your potential and create the life you've always wanted."

— Mel Robbins, *New York Times* bestselling author, *The High 5 Habit*, and host of the award-winning *The Mel Robbins Podcast*

"A wonderful book on the power of a peak morning routine to deliver the consistently excellent days that make a truly amazing life."

— Robin Sharma, #1 worldwide bestselling author, *The Monk Who Sold His Ferrari*, and *The 5AM Club*

"Hal Elrod is a genius, and his book *The Miracle Morning* has been magical in my life. What Hal has done with his acronym S.A.V.E.R.S. is taken the *best practices* developed over centuries of human consciousness development and condensed the 'best of the best' into a daily morning ritual. A ritual that is now part of my day."

— Robert Kiyosaki, bestselling author, *Rich Dad Poor Dad*—the #1 personal finance book of all time

"As a mom, entrepreneur, and professional athlete, *The Miracle Morning* has been the one routine that has enabled me to show up at my best every day, regardless of which role I'm in."

— Laila Ali, 18-time undefeated world champion boxer and American television personality

"Hal Elrod has lived a life that would break most people, but somehow he has managed to turn all of his tragedies into a perspective that has allowed him to be incredibly successful in both his personal and professional life. He is a reminder to all of us that if we're willing to do the work, we are capable of true greatness, even when the deck is stacked against us."

— Tom Bilyeu, innovative entrepreneur; host and producer of *Impact Theory*; coach, speaker; and award-winning screenwriter

"Read *The Miracle Morning* so you can become the person you need to be to create the life you truly want. It's time. You deserve this."

— JJ Virgin, *New York Times* bestselling author, *The Virgin Diet*, and host of the *Well Beyond 40 With JJ Virgin* podcast

"I've known Hal for many years. After surviving multiple near-death experiences and helping millions of people transform their lives with his books, he is living proof that we can all overcome our challenges to create the life and make the impact we want to make in the world. This book shows you how."

— Lewis Howes, *New York Times* bestselling author, *The Greatness Mindset*

"One of my favorite things about Hal is how much he cares about other people. *The Miracle Morning* was born from that compassion, and the reason it's gone from a book to a movement is that it comes from Hal's heart. If you're one of the people who hasn't read this book yet, then what are you waiting for? It may change more than your mornings. It may actually change your entire life."

— Joe Polish, founder of Genius Network and *Wall Street Journal* bestselling author, *What's In It for Them?*

"I know of no kinder, more compassionate person than Hal Elrod, and that compassion shines through every page of this book. *The Miracle Morning* has become a phenomenon not only because of Hal''s practical approach but also because of the sincerity of his mission. Read this if you want your mornings and your life to be miraculous!"

— Anna David, *New York Times* bestselling author of eight books, including *The Miracle Morning for Addiction Recovery*

"*The Miracle Morning* is a proven method for personal transformation and one that I've not only used in my own life but that I've had Hal teach to my students. Read this book, and you'll gain the ability to optimize every aspect of your life."

— Dr. Benjamin Hardy, psychologist and author, *Be Your Future Self Now*

"One of the greatest steps you can take to improve your health is to master your morning routine. *The Miracle Morning* is the go-to book I recommend to everyone to learn an effective step-by-step process to transform your life before the sun comes up! I love Hal's heart, his mission, and his desire to heal the world one morning at a time!"

— Dr. Mindy Pelz, international bestselling author, *Fast Like a Girl*, and *The Menopause Reset*

"If you are going to listen to what anyone has to say about miracles, it should be Hal Elrod."

— Dave Asprey, founder of Bulletproof Coffee, and four-time *New York Times* bestselling author, including *The Bulletproof Diet*, and *Super Human*

"I've been following Hal Elrod's words, his life, his inspiration, ever since he first began writing about *The Miracle Morning*. After changing the lives of millions, including my own, it is truly a gift Hal has given us by writing this new and expanded edition. *The Miracle Morning* has truly changed my life."

— James Altucher, *Wall Street Journal* bestselling author of *Choose Yourself*, and host of *The James Altucher Show*

"A morning practice can be foundational for the success you want to create in your life. *The Miracle Morning* will enable you to develop the habits you'll come to rely on as you live into your vision."

— Honorée Corder, publishing strategist, author of 50+ books, including *Write Your First Nonfiction Book*

"The first thing on my calendar each day is my Miracle Morning routine. I can't even begin to tell you how much this daily ritual has transformed my life. It's simple, science-backed, and the results will speak for themselves! If you want to take control of your life and write the story YOU want, *The Miracle Morning* is your blueprint to do it."

— Shawn Stevenson, bestselling author, *Eat Smarter* and *Sleep Smarter*

"Hal Elrod is someone who walks his talk and has overcome insurmountable challenges, proving that you can do the same and live the life of your dreams. Give yourself the gift of reading *The Miracle Morning* and create the life you want!"

— Neka Pasquale, founder and Chief Product Officer at Urban Remedy

"Fellow seekers of enlightenment, allow me to speak of one who has dedicated his life to the elevation of humanity's consciousness. Hal Elrod has authored many illuminating works, but his latest is truly a masterpiece. What strikes me most is that Hal writes as if he's speaking directly to you. It's as though we were sitting together, chatting over a warm cup of tea, and I asked him how to transform my life. This book is his answer, my friend. Within its pages lies the roadmap to unlocking your true potential and creating the life you desire by illuminating the path to your true self. Through his teachings, millions have been empowered to harness their power within and elevate their consciousness each and every day. Hal Elrod is a beacon of light in this world, guiding us all toward a brighter future. Embrace his wisdom in this sacred text and unlock your true potential, and let it transform your life as it has mine."

— Drew Canole, father, and founder and CEO of Organifi

"*The Miracle Morning* is an important book because everyone's morning is important, and not always at the same time. Hal has looked at the science, made some of his own discoveries, and worked with me to improve his sleep, which we see reflected in this awesome updated version. As a top sleep expert, I see this as a critical step in everyone's overall health. I am especially excited to see the new section on elevating consciousness one morning at a time. This is how dreams really do come true, and I should know as The Sleep Doctor."

— **Michael J Breus, PhD, founder of thesleepdoctor.com**

"The next best thing to knowing Hal Elrod personally is reading one of his books. Reading *The Miracle Morning* is like having Hal by your side, helping you transform your life."

— **Codie Sanchez, founder of Contrarian Thinking**

"*The Miracle Morning* sets you up for success in every area of your life by giving you a simple, proven framework for personal development, even if you don't consider yourself to be a morning person."

— **Dan Martell, WSJ bestselling author, *Buy Back Your Time***

"Ever since I read this book, I have devoted my morning routine to include everything Hal teaches. *The Miracle Morning* has been nothing short of transformative for me. It will do the same for you. Everything you need is in this book. Your best life starts now."

— **Mike Michalowicz, bestselling author, *Profit First* and *All In***

"*The Miracle Morning* has been the key to loving my life, feeling fulfilled, and developing skills, self-awareness, and personal power. By starting my day this way, I've created more abundance and handled some of the most difficult circumstances and times. My life is filled with more wealth thanks to *The Miracle Morning*."

— **Garrett Gunderson, *New York Times* and *Wall Street Journal* bestselling author**

"The millions of people who have already transformed their lives after reading *The Miracle Morning* prove that you can change your life simply by changing the way you start your day. And anything Hal does is a game-changer because his heart is so good."

— **Cathy Heller, bestselling author of *Don't Keep Your Day Job*, and host of *The Cathy Heller Podcast***

"I've always been a night owl, so the idea of creating a morning routine was never an option and didn't appeal to me. Things were already going well with my current schedule, so why fix it if it's not broken? But I kept hearing about how valuable people's morning routines are to their personal lives and professional success. So, I made a commitment to give *The Miracle Morning* a shot. I've been doing it for several years now and have seen massive positive changes in my focus, in my mood, and in how much I'm able to get done."

— **Pat Flynn**, *Wall Street Journal* **bestselling author of** *Will It Fly?* **and host of the** *Smart Passive Income* **podcast**

"Hal has helped millions of people with *The Miracle Morning*. Not only has it shifted those who've read it, but its impact has been amplified due to enabling the readers to show up at their best for others. This one book will enable you to get the most out of your life so that you can help the people you love and those you lead to do the same."

— **Cameron Herold**, **author of** *Vivid Vision* **and** *The Second In Command*, **co-author of** *The Miracle Morning for Entrepreneurs*

"Hal Elrod has faced seemingly insurmountable obstacles, and yet he found a way to overcome all of them and achieve extraordinary goals. In *The Miracle Morning*, you will learn how YOU can overcome your challenges and accomplish everything you want in your life."

— **Vasavi Kumar**, **voiceover artist and author of** *Say It Out Loud*

"If you study the world's most successful people, you'll find that one of the keys to their success is that they start their day with a structured morning routine. *The Miracle Morning* will enable you to do the same, even if you've never considered yourself to be a morning person."

— **Rob Dial**, **host of** *The Mindset Mentor* **podcast and author of** *Level Up*

"WOW! If you are looking to improve your life, this is a must-read. Hal does a masterful job outlining the foundation for the ideal morning routine and shows the reader how it's simple to implement. Changed the game for me, and I am fully confident it will for you as well!"

— **David Nurse**, **world-renowned mindset specialist, WSJ bestselling author, Top 50 ranked keynote speaker (Real Leaders)**

"I'm not a 'morning person,' but *The Miracle Morning* gave me the tools I was missing to build a better life by building better mornings. Read the book . . . even if you hate mornings."

— **Ryan Deiss**, **entrepreneur, investor, and founder of three Inc. 5000 companies, including DigitalMarketer.com and The Scalable Company**

"Want to activate your heroic potential and wake up every morning ready to make TODAY a masterpiece?! Hal Elrod is THE guide to help you do it. Hal's original version of *The Miracle Morning* changed my life and deeply inspired my work. This updated and expanded edition is even more powerful. Get this book. Read it. Apply the wisdom in it. And change your life—starting tomorrow morning."

— Brian Johnson, founder and CEO of Heroic, author of
ARETÉ: Activate Your Heroic Potential

"Growing up I was fueled by an extraordinary ambition, but my performance in school fell short, so I was constantly seeking ways to improve. Despite eventually tasting success, I remain relentless in my pursuit of self-improvement. Today, *The Miracle Morning* is one of the few books I still regularly revisit whenever I find myself off course, as we all do, to remind me what I need to do to get where I want to go."

— Dan Caldwell, co-founder of the global combat sports
brand TapouT, host of *The Pretty and Punk Podcast*

"*The Miracle Morning* is THE FORMULA for creating a miraculous life. I have shared Hal's powerful morning ritual with my students worldwide for over 12 years. I love the S.A.V.E.R.S., which have been instrumental in helping me manifest my dreams. Read the book, implement what you learn, and watch all of your dreams begin to manifest. *The Miracle Morning* is truly the gift that keeps on giving."

— Dashama, founder of Flow State Institute and Bright Mind Foundation,
author of *Journey to Joyful,* creator of the 30-Day Yoga Challenge™h

"Every time I hang out with Hal and his family, I'm always reminded that creating a life filled with happiness, success, and fulfillment doesn't accidentally happen. If you are ready to create that kind of life, *The Miracle Morning* is a masterful guide that shows you how."

— JP Sears, husband, father, author, and comedian

"This may be the most important book you ever read because it sets you up to win every day. And that is how you create an extraordinary life—one morning and one day at a time."

— Jairek Robbins, author, *Live It!,* and award-winning performance coach

"By picking up this book and implementing what composes a Miracle Morning that Hal Elrod so eloquently outlines, you could completely change your life. *The Miracle Morning* is not only an essential and brilliant way to start your day; it is also the beginning of a totally new life and new you."

—Mark Groves, founder of Create The Love, co-author, *Liberated Love*

Also by Hal Elrod

The Miracle Equation
Taking Life Head On

The Miracle Morning Series

The Miracle Morning for Salespeople
The Miracle Morning for Real Estate Agents
The Miracle Morning for Network Marketers
The Miracle Morning for Parents and Families
The Miracle Morning Art of Affirmations
The Miracle Morning for Entrepreneurs
The Miracle Morning Millionaires
The Miracle Morning for Addiction Recovery
The Miracle Morning for Couples
The Miracle Morning for Transforming Your Relationship
The Miracle Morning for Teachers
The Miracle Morning for College Students
The Miracle Morning Journal
The Miracle Morning Companion Planner

the

MIRACLE MORNING

UPDATED AND EXPANDED EDITION

The Not-So-Obvious Secret Guaranteed
to Transform Your Life (Before 8 AM)

HAL ELROD

BenBella Books, Inc.
Dallas, TX

BenBella

BenBella Books, Inc.
10440 N. Central Expressway
Suite 800
Dallas, TX 75231
benbellabooks.com
Send feedback to feedback@benbellabooks.com

BenBella is a federally registered trademark.

Printed in the United States of America
10 9 8 7 6 5 4 3 2

Library of Congress Control Number: 2023942648
ISBN 9781637744345 (print)
ISBN 9781637744352 (ebook)

Editing by Joel D and Sue Canfield, SomedayBox.com, and Glenn Yeffeth
Revisions by Elaine Pofeldt, ElainePofeldt.com, and Emily Klein, KleinWriter.com
Copyediting by Jessica Easto
Proofreading by Lisa Story and Cape Cod Compositors, Inc.
Text design by Aaron Edmiston
Text composition by PerfecType, Nashville, TN
Cover design by Ty Nowicki
Cover image © Adobe Stock / Iuliia (sun icon) and Shcherbyna (background)
Printed by Lake Book Manufacturing

Dedicated to Ursula, my wife-for-life, my muse,
and the most extraordinary person I know.

To Sophia and Halsten, you are the greatest blessings in my
life, and being your dad means more to me than anything.

CONTENTS

FOREWORD

H al Elrod is a genius and his book *The Miracle Morning* has been magical in my life.

I have been in the human potential / personal development movement since 1973, when I did my first EST training and saw a whole new world of possibilities. Since then, I have studied religions, prayer, meditation, yoga, affirmation, visualization, and NLP (neurolinguistic programming). I've walked on fire, and explored other "unconventional" philosophies, some "too far out there" to mention.

What Hal has done with his acronym S.A.V.E.R.S. is taken the *best practices*—developed over centuries of human consciousness development—and condensed the "best of the best" into a daily morning ritual. A ritual that is now part of my day.

Many people do *one* of the S.A.V.E.R.S daily. For example, many people do the *E*; they *exercise* every morning. Others do *S* for *silence* or meditation, or *S* for *scribing*, journaling every morning. But until Hal packaged S.A.V.E.R.S., no one was doing all six ancient best practices every morning.

The Miracle Morning is perfect for very busy, successful people. Going through S.A.V.E.R.S. every morning is like pumping rocket fuel into my body, mind, and spirit . . . *before* I start my day, every day.

As my rich dad often said, "I can always make another dollar, but I cannot make another day." If you want to maximize every day of your life, read *The Miracle Morning*.

Robert Kiyosaki

Robert Kiyosaki is the *New York Times* bestselling author of the #1 personal finance book of all time, *Rich Dad Poor Dad*, and founder of the financial education–based Rich Dad Company.

WHAT'S NEW?

Dramatic Upgrades to This Expanded Edition

When I made the decision to create a morning ritual back in 2008, during the Great Recession, I did so because I was desperate. I had lost over half of my income and was struggling in almost every area of my life. Although I had never been and never really believed I could become a "morning person," I started waking up earlier and implemented six of the most timeless, proven personal development practices in an attempt to turn my life around. It never even crossed my mind that it might one day become a book, let alone help millions of people.

This is my 15th consecutive year practicing the six-step morning ritual that I teach in this book, an average of six to seven days a week. (My preference is seven, but my wife's preference is to keep me up way past my bedtime during our weekly date nights.) I've also benefited from more than a decade of interacting with and learning from members of the Miracle Morning Community. As someone who is mildly obsessed with optimizing nearly every aspect of my life, I've learned *a lot* since I wrote the original book, and I've incorporated those lessons into this edition.

I've also read thousands of the more than 50,000 online reviews for the book across platforms like Amazon, Audible, and Goodreads, to look for common themes. I've always wanted to understand which aspects resonate with readers, as well as those that don't, so that I can address any issues and make improvements.

As a result of my personal evolution and feedback and requests from readers and Miracle Morning practitioners, I've made significant revisions to every chapter and nearly every page of this book. Additionally, I've focused on answering questions that people had after reading the original version and implementing the practice, such as:

- *What if I've never been a "morning person" and don't believe I can become one?*
- *What if I've been doing the Miracle Morning for a long time and it's starting to feel stale; how do I make it exciting again?*
- *What if I'm not motivated and already feel so overwhelmed that I can't imagine adding anything else to my schedule/ life?*
- *How can I use my Miracle Morning to achieve specific goals or overcome difficult challenges that I'm facing?*

I've also included two brand new, never-before-published chapters: "Chapter 11: The Miracle Evening" and "Chapter 12: The Miracle Life."

"The Miracle Evening" will give you a comprehensive, step-by-step plan for establishing an evening ritual that is designed to help you fall asleep feeling genuinely grateful, happy, and at peace, especially when life is difficult and you're feeling stressed and overwhelmed.

"The Miracle Life" will teach you how to elevate your consciousness to a state of Inner Freedom so that you can proactively take control of how you feel and experience every moment of your life, regardless of your circumstances and particularly when life is difficult.

Whether you are new to *The Miracle Morning*, or you've read the original book (even multiple times), I wrote this Updated and Expanded edition to meet the needs and exceed the expectations of readers at every level. I hope this new version and the stories and lessons contained within enable you to love the life you have and create the most extraordinary life that you can imagine. You deserve nothing less.

A New Miracle Morning Mission: Elevating the Consciousness of Humanity, One Morning and One Person at a Time

When I self-published *The Miracle Morning* on December 12, 2012, I did so with the conviction that I had a responsibility to share the morning routine that changed my life with as many people as possible. Having seen the profound impact that the book and, more accurately, the Miracle Morning *routine* made in people's lives, my sense of responsibility grew. I started thinking bigger and eventually committed to a personal mission: *Change one million lives, one morning at a time.*

Although *one million* was somewhat of an arbitrary number, it felt so significant that it stretched my imagination beyond what I considered to be probable. As an unknown, self-published author, I had no idea how to reach a million people. But I figured it would give me a meaningful goal to work toward that year and possibly for the rest of my life.

It took roughly six years of maintaining unwavering faith and extraordinary effort to get the book into the hands of more than one million people. During that time, I was also diagnosed with cancer and given a 30 percent chance of surviving (more on that later). Thankfully, the mission was no longer dependent on me. While I was focused on beating cancer, the Miracle Morning had evolved into a global community and a worldwide movement. As readers consistently experienced profound personal transformations, they shared their experiences and the book with others. This resulted in the manuscript being translated and published in 37 languages and reaching millions of people spread throughout more than one hundred countries.

The mission that began as changing one million lives, one morning at a time, has grown into something that is far more significant and imperative to the future of humanity, and it is no longer just my own. It has become apparent that when you dedicate time to a daily Miracle Morning practice, you elevate your consciousness by becoming more aware and intentional about how your thoughts, words, and actions impact your life and the lives of every person you interact with. As each of us elevates our own consciousness, we are collectively **elevating the consciousness of humanity, one morning and one person at a time**. Thus, the collective impact that is being made by millions of Miracle Morning practitioners is meaningfully affecting the lives of tens of millions and soon to be hundreds of millions of other people.

Now, more than ever, I believe it's imperative for us to remember that we are all members of the human family and will always have infinitely more in common than the perceived differences that far too many people cling to. As a part of my family, I love and appreciate you more than you know. I am deeply grateful to be on this mission with you at this unique time in human history. Humanity needs us. Let's make every morning count.

A NOTE TO YOU

How This Book Will Transform Your Life

Chances are we've never met, and I certainly don't know what your life is like right now. You could be experiencing extraordinary levels of success and fulfillment. Or you could be enduring one of the most difficult times of your life. I have no idea.

Still, I believe there are at least a few things that we can be pretty certain we have in common. Probably more than just a few, but this will give us some common ground to start with. First, *we want to improve our lives and ourselves*. This is not to suggest that there is anything *wrong* with us or our lives, but as human beings, we were born with the innate desire and drive to continuously grow and improve. I believe it's within all of us. Yet, most of us wake up each day, and life pretty much stays the same. Life stays the same because we stay the same. As you'll discover in the following pages, transforming your life is most easily accomplished by first dedicating time to transforming yourself. As you get better, day by day, morning by morning, your life inevitably will get better.

Second, *we've faced adversity throughout our lives, and there is more we can expect to face in the future*. Life can be difficult, unfair, painful, and push the limits of being utterly unbearable. However, if we can maintain the perspective that every adversity we face is an opportunity for us to learn, grow, and become better than we've ever been, then the greater our adversity, the greater our destiny.

If you take an inventory of your past experiences, you might realize that in the end things usually work out the way they're supposed to. And sometimes they work out even better than we could have imagined. Think about any challenges you've ever faced that, at the time, may have seemed insurmountable or unbearable. Think of something—a breakup, a lost job, the death of a loved one, or anything else that caused you to experience excessive mental, emotional, or physical pain. Didn't you get through every single one of them? I'm not talking about the ones that you are still dealing with right now (although those will likely work out for the best as well, and possibly better than you can imagine). I'm talking about every single difficult experience that you've ever faced throughout your life. You have a 100 percent track record of getting through all of them, which is a pretty good indicator that you'll be able to get through every adversity you experience in the future.

That is why, no matter how hopeless some aspects of our lives may seem, we must remember that circumstances are always changing and that we can handle any challenge we're faced with. To do this, you must be willing to accept responsibility for every aspect of your life from this point forward and refuse to give away your power by blaming anyone else. While blame may be useful in determining who is at fault for something, it is only when we are willing to accept responsibility for *everything* in our lives that we harness our ability to change or create *anything* in our lives.

Wherever you are in your life right now is both temporary and exactly where you are supposed to be. You have arrived at this moment to learn what you must so you can become the person you need to be to create the life you truly want. Even when life is difficult or seems hopeless, the present is always an opportunity for us to learn, grow, and become better than we've ever been before.

You are in the process of writing your life story, and no good story is without a hero or heroine overcoming their fair share of challenges. In fact, the bigger the challenges, the better the story. Since there are no restrictions and no limits to where your story goes from here, what do you want your next chapter to be about?

The good news is that you have the ability to change—or create—anything in your life, starting right now. I'm not saying it won't require effort, but you can immediately begin the process by dedicating time each day to develop the capabilities you need to do so. That's what this book is about, giving you a daily practice that will ensure you become the person you need to be to create and experience everything you have ever wanted for your life. Get excited because there are very few limits as to what's going to become possible for you.

If you are in the midst of adversity, whether it's personal or professional, mental, emotional, physical, financial, relational, or anything else, I want you to know that the Miracle Morning has enabled people from all walks of life to overcome seemingly insurmountable challenges, make major breakthroughs, and turn their circumstances around, often in a very short period of time.

A profound example of this is Keith Minick, former director of business operations at Turner Broadcasting System. After his son died and he suffered from depression for over a year, he says that his very first Miracle Morning changed everything. I'll let Keith tell you in his words:

In May of 2012, my son, Everett, passed away after living three short but tremendously impactful hours. It was the hardest thing I have ever been through. Between his death and dissatisfaction at my job, I found myself in a state of depression. It just didn't seem like I could make any progress in life and get through feeling down on myself. It wasn't for lack of trying; I read many of the most popular self-help books out there, but nothing really clicked for me until I found the Miracle Morning.

I heard Hal Elrod on a podcast and instantly became intrigued. I purchased the book and read it in one day. The next day would change my life forever. I set my alarm, got up, and began the S.A.V.E.R.S. framework. I experienced instant changes in my psychology, physiology, and mental health. I took ownership of where I was and set forward a path and a process to achieve the life I wanted, which was reaffirmed in my vision board and affirmations every day. Since the Miracle Morning, I left my position at Turner, started two businesses, sold one, and I'm truly living my best life.

I have been practicing the Miracle Morning routine for nearly a decade. The S.A.V.E.R.S. framework continues to be a major part of my life. A major factor to my success has been implementing, maintaining, and evolving my routine. I encourage anyone looking for a breakthrough, struggling with depression, or trying to get unstuck in life to read and implement the S.A.V.E.R.S. framework.

Keith's story is a real-life example of just how fast life can change for you and how, even a decade later, you can still be evolving into the best version of yourself.

If, on the other hand, you are already sustaining meaningful levels of success, the Miracle Morning has proven to help high achievers break through to that elusive *next level* and take their personal and professional results beyond what they've achieved in the past. While *your* next level may include increasing your income, advancing your career, or growing your business, progress is often more about discovering new ways to experience deeper levels of fulfillment and balance in the most important areas of your life, which you may have neglected up until this point. This can mean making significant improvements to your physical or mental health, happiness, relationships, spirituality, or any other priorities.

Whether you want to make major improvements in just a few key areas, or you are ready for a complete overhaul that can radically transform your entire life—so that your current circumstance will soon become only a memory of how things used to be—you've picked up the right book. You are about to embark on a miraculous journey, using a revolutionary process made up of six daily habits that are guaranteed to enhance any—or every—area of your life.

I do realize that these are big promises to make, but I can say this with confidence because I've read thousands of letters and reviews from readers who've told me that reading this book and implementing what they learned transformed their lives in meaningful ways, and often very quickly. It's worked for all types of people, regardless of age, race, gender, location, circumstances, and even socioeconomic status. It can absolutely be the one thing that enables you to make the changes you've wanted to experience in your life.

I encourage you to read just a few short excerpts from some of the letters I've received to help you consider what's possible for you. These are real-life stories from people, just like you and me, who read this book and then used the Miracle Morning routine to transform their lives.

"Finding the Miracle Morning is one of the best things that has happened in my life. I have been a dedicated practitioner for nearly 12 months. Prior to reading the book, I was unfit and rapidly losing strength, unhappy, undisciplined, and not living my values. Much of life felt wrong. I cried most days. Then I found the Miracle Morning. What a complete blessing. The positive journey began. 12 months later, I feel fit, strong, purposeful, focused, present, and much happier. As a mother of three teenage daughters and the owner of two small businesses (which my husband and I run), I am very busy. The Miracle Morning keeps me focused and on track. One of the best things about the Miracle Morning is the community. I feel like I have finally found my tribe—people who love continuous learning and self-improvement. I am so grateful to you, Hal."

—Katrina Kelly (1 year practicing the Miracle Morning)

"My wife, Yatra, and I began practicing the Miracle Morning in December 2016. We had both just gone through the hardest transition of our lives and were at a very low point. We closed our restaurant, Yatra was laid off while on maternity leave, and for the first time, we were both unemployed with a mountain of debt. We began the S.A.V.E.R.S. framework, and within weeks we started seeing results. We had a more positive mindset, and new opportunities, both personally and professionally, started to present themselves. *The Miracle Morning* literally changed our lives and pulled us out of the funk we were in, and I am forever grateful to Hal for that! I am a father of three boys, have a beautiful wife of 14 years, and now run a successful and growing business!"

—Christopher Moscarino (5 years practicing the Miracle Morning)

"I'm a real estate agent, married, and a mother of three. My biggest struggle was blocking out time for myself. My life was missing balance and self-care. I had carved out time for everything and everyone but not for my own mental health. The Miracle Morning changed my life and my business within the first six months, literally doubling my income. This morning routine changed me and my daily perspective because I took the time to start my day with purpose. For the first time since being a teenager, I was the center of my morning, not my kids or work. This shift in perception changed everything for me. I've gifted the book to over 15 people, anytime they ask, "How do you it? What's your secret?" The Miracle Morning is my secret. It's my foundation for my daily routine. I feel like I finally got the memo and figured out the key to living a balanced life. Thanks, Hal."

—**Maria Rita Velez (2 years practicing the Miracle Morning)**

"I have been doing the Miracle Morning for a little over four years. I have had many accomplishments over that time with my career, but the one that is most important to me is recent and very personal. Two people very close to me have been struggling with anxiety and depression, one of them with suicidal thoughts. This sent me into a bit of a spiral of guilt, blaming myself, and a little of my own depression. Thanks to the Miracle Morning Community, practice, and leaning into my morning routine, I was able to get my mental health back quickly and be there for those I love and help them through this. I know that as long as I stay consistent and fully engaged with my S.A.V.E.R.S. routine, I can stay strong for those I love as they go through difficult times. Hal Elrod, thank you for everything you have done with the Miracle Morning. It is making a difference this world needs."

—**Rob Stein (4 years practicing the Miracle Morning)**

"The Miracle Morning has given purpose to the start of my day. It's given me the tools to prioritize 'me' time before my son and husband get out of bed. As an entrepreneur, it's increased my productivity and profitability through the simple but powerful habit of the Miracle Morning. It also gave me the power to quit smoking after more than 25 years. Overall, my life is better, and I am more balanced because of it."

—**Jennifer Cooper (3 years practicing the Miracle Morning)**

The experiences of these readers aren't unique and have become the norm for anyone who practices the Miracle Morning. They are evidence of what's possible for you when you simply commit to reading this book—all the way to the end—and implementing the steps outlined within.

I invite you to pause for a moment and take a deep breath as we are about to embark on a journey together, one that will invite you to tap into your innate human desire and drive to create the most fulfilling life you can imagine. I'm speaking of a life in which you are truly at peace, genuinely happy, and actively creating the impact you want to make in the world. That life is always available to you, simply waiting for you to wake up to your full potential so that you can claim it. This book shows you how.

With Love & Gratitude,

Hal

A SPECIAL INVITATION

to the Miracle Morning Community

THE MIRACLE MORNING COMMUNITY

Millions of like-minded individuals, from around the world, who wake up each day to fulfill their potential while helping others do the same.

If you'd like to connect with and get support from other like-minded Miracle Morning practitioners as you read this book, whether to ask questions or just observe and learn from how they're approaching their practice, I invite you to join the **Miracle Morning Community**.

What began as a Facebook group with me, my parents, and five of my friends has grown into an online community with over 300,000 members from more than one hundred countries. It's always free to join, and while you'll find many people who are just beginning their Miracle Morning journey, you'll also find those who have been practicing for years and who will happily share advice, support, and guidance to help you accelerate your success.

As the author of *The Miracle Morning*, I wanted to create a space where we can all come together to connect, ask questions, share best practices, support one another, discuss the book, post videos, find an accountability partner, and even swap smoothie recipes and exercise routines. I never imagined that the Miracle Morning Community would become one of the most positive, engaged, and supportive online communities in the world, but it truly has!

You can begin connecting with other Miracle Morning practitioners. Just visit MiracleMorningCommunity.com and request to join. I check in regularly (almost every single day), posting content and engaging in the comments, so I look forward to seeing you there!

Miracle Morning Community Resources: The App and the Movie

There are two additional resources (both of which are free) that can help you as you begin your Miracle Morning journey: the Miracle Morning Routine app and *The Miracle Morning* movie.

The single most requested resource by members of the Miracle Morning Community has been a mobile app to track your Miracle Mornings and help you become consistent and accountable. Additional features include a built-in journal with writing prompts, an affirmations creator, customizable timers, and optional guided audio tracks to lead you through the S.A.V.E.R.S. (silence, affirmations, visualization, exercise, reading, and scribing) so that you can complete your Miracle Morning by simply clicking "play" and following along. The app is available for both iPhone and Android at **MiracleMorning.com/app**.

Filmed over the course of six years, *The Miracle Morning* movie is an inspiring feature-length documentary that goes beyond the book and actually shows you how people are transforming their lives, one morning at a time. It also takes you into the homes of world-renowned authors, doctors, scientists, entrepreneurs, and professional athletes to reveal how these highly productive individuals start their day. It also takes you into one of the most difficult times of my life. Two years into filming, I was unexpectedly diagnosed with a rare form of cancer and given a 30 percent chance of surviving. Our director kept the cameras rolling in order to capture my mindset and the holistic approach I used to beat cancer in hopes that it might inspire someone else who is battling cancer or some other disease. You can watch the extended trailer and access the full film at **MiracleMorning.com/movie**.

So far, the app has a rating of 4.9 out of 5.0 stars and the movie has a rating of 4.6 out of 5.0 stars, so I hope these free resources are as helpful for you as they've been for others!

Welcome to the Miracle Morning Community!

"There are only two ways to live your life. One is as though nothing is a miracle. The other is as though everything is a miracle."
—Albert Einstein

"Miracles do not happen in contradiction with nature, but in contradiction with what we know about nature."
—Saint Augustine

"Each morning we are born again. What we do today is what matters most."
—Buddha

INTRODUCTION

How to Transform Adversity into Opportunity

On December 3rd, 1999, my life was good. Actually, it was *great*. At 20 years old, my first year of college was behind me, and I had spent the last 18 months pursuing an unlikely career choice, becoming one of the top sales reps for an international cutlery company—Cutco. Thanks to the combined support of a mentor and my family, I had broken numerous company sales records and was earning more money than I ever imagined I could earn at that age.

I was also in a loving, committed relationship with a girl whom I adored and had a supportive family and the best friends a guy could ask for. I felt truly blessed. You might say I was on top of the world—which is why there was no way I could have ever anticipated that this was the night my world would end.

11:32 PM / Driving 70 mph Southbound on Highway 99

Maybe it was for the best, but I don't recall seeing the headlights barreling down the highway directly toward my car. What I experienced in those moments leading up to the crash is still a mystery to me. In fact, I'm not clear as to where the stories told to me by friends and family end and my actual memories begin. It's all a bit of a blur. I only know the following details from reading police reports, talking with eyewitnesses, and reviewing my medical records.

It was December 3, a chilly winter night in Northern California. I was driving home after having given a speech at the Nor Cal division conference for Cutco. I had received my first ever standing ovation, and I was on cloud nine!

I was driving a Ford Mustang when suddenly a full-size Chevy Silverado truck, driven by a drunk driver, crossed the center line on the highway and crashed head-on into my car at over 80 miles per hour. The metal frames of our two vehicles collided—screaming and screeching as they twisted and broke. Inside the cabin, the Mustang's airbags exploded with enough force to render me unconscious and concussed. My brain, still traveling at 70 miles per hour, smashed into the front of my skull, destroying much of the vital tissue that comprised my frontal lobe. But the worst was yet to come.

The impact point of the head-on collision was off-center and sent my car spinning out of control into oncoming traffic. A second vehicle—a Saturn sedan traveling over 70 miles per hour—crashed into my driver's side door. The left door of my Mustang collapsed and crushed the left side of my body, breaking 11 bones. My femur—the largest bone in the human body—snapped in half with such force that one end speared through the skin of my thigh and tore a hole in the black dress slacks that I had worn for my speech. My humerus bone, concealed beneath my left bicep, suffered a similar fate, breaking into two halves, one of which pierced through my skin. My left elbow shattered into pieces. The radial nerve in my forearm was severed, cutting off communication between my brain and my left hand. My left ear was also nearly severed, remaining attached to my head by less than an inch of skin. My left eye socket was shattered, leaving my eyeball unsupported. The frame of the metal roof caved in on my head, slicing a V into the top of my skull. Lastly, my pelvis was given the challenge of separating the car door and the center console and failed, fracturing in three separate places.

All of this took place in a matter of seconds. As the Mustang rolled to a stop, the full moon shone overhead and illuminated the graphic scene. I was bleeding from the top of my head down to the gaping holes in my arm and leg. And I was trapped. The contorted metal frame of the Mustang's door was pressed firmly against the left side of my body. Unable to withstand the unbearable pain, in an automated process of self-preservation, my body shut itself down, and I slipped into a coma.

My best friend, Jeremy, who had left the conference just minutes after I had, arrived at the gruesome scene. Jeremy pulled his car off to the side of the road and rushed to check on me. What he's described to me is like something out of a horror movie. As he approached the side of my car, he found me lifeless, my face mangled and covered in blood. He called out to me repeatedly, but I was unresponsive. He checked my pulse, told me to hang on, and dialed 9-1-1.

You Only Live . . . Twice?

What happened next was nothing short of incredible—and what some have called a *miracle*. The fire department and paramedics arrived at the scene and worked determinedly to get me out of the car while attempting to stabilize me. Time was of the essence as I was losing blood. After 50 minutes of attempting to remove me from my vehicle, they were finally able to use the Jaws of Life to pry the roof back and pull me out. I was bleeding out. My heart stopped beating, and I stopped breathing. Clinically, I was dead.

Paramedics rushed my lifeless body into the back of a medical evacuation helicopter that had arrived to airlift me to the nearest hospital. They hooked me up to an IV, administered CPR, and used a defibrillator to deliver doses of electric current to my heart. After six drawn-out minutes without a heartbeat, they brought me back to life. The uphill battle to survive was just beginning.

I spent the next six days in a coma in critical condition. During that time, I flatlined twice more. My poor parents never left my side, feeling helpless and fearing the worst as they watched me fight for my life. They had already lost one child. When I was eight years old, my baby sister, Amery, died of heart failure, just 18 months after she was born. After losing their youngest, my parents were now facing the possibility of losing me, their firstborn.

I underwent multiple surgeries to repair my broken bones by fastening them to titanium rods, had screws inserted into my elbow, and replaced the shattered bones in my eye socket with titanium plates. When I finally woke from the coma and was told what happened, I was faced with an unimaginable reality. Trying to process what had happened to me was surreal, to say the least. But what was arguably the most difficult news to hear was the doctors' prognosis that I was most likely never going to walk again. From their vantage point, I would spend the rest of my life in a wheelchair.

Accepting my newfound circumstances was truly incomprehensible to me. However, everything that had happened up until this point was now out of my control, and I was left with an unavoidable choice. It is the only choice any of us have when we are facing adversity: *How am I going to respond?*

Our Perspectives Dictate Our Reality

Coming to grips with my new reality wasn't easy. Being told I may never walk again and envisioning what my life was going to be like was certainly difficult to process. The consequence of my brain damage—constantly forgetting where I was, what happened five minutes ago, or what was said from moment to moment—was similarly discouraging. I also didn't have use of my left hand, and doctors didn't know if I'd ever get it back. Then there was my fractured left eye socket, which had been repaired and bandaged, but the doctors said that when they removed the bandage, I might be permanently blind in my left eye.

Late at night, after my visitors had left, was the most difficult time for me. I would lay awake, listening to the beeping of the medical equipment that was monitoring my vital signs, feeling afraid and overwhelmed by it all. *Would I spend the rest of my life in a wheelchair? Would other people have to take care of me? Would I ever be able to live on my own again? Would I still be able to pursue my goals? Why did this happen to me? I didn't do anything to deserve this. This isn't fair!*

Soon enough, though, I realized that this victim mentality wasn't serving me and that there was no point in feeling sorry for myself. The only logical choice I had—that any of us have—was to accept reality exactly as it was, be at peace with what I couldn't change, be grateful for what I had, and take responsibility for actively creating the life I wanted, despite my current circumstances. I concluded that if the doctors were right and I was going to spend the rest of my life in a wheelchair, I could either allow myself to be miserable or I could choose to be happy. Either way, I would be in a wheelchair. So, I decided that I would choose to be the happiest, most grateful person that anyone had ever seen in a wheelchair.

I also decided that I didn't have to passively succumb to the prognosis that I would never walk again. *What if the doctors were wrong?* While I chose to be at peace with the worst-case scenario so that it had no power over my mental and emotional state, I simultaneously focused all my energy on creating the outcomes that I wanted. I visualized myself walking. I imagined my body healing. I prayed for strength and for a miracle. And I did the work. I rolled up to physical therapy in my wheelchair every day and enthusiastically proclaimed to my therapists that I was going to walk again!

After three challenging and painful weeks of recovery and rehabilitation, living full-time in the hospital, one of my doctors entered my room with the routine X-rays he had ordered the day before. With a puzzled tone and expression, he explained that my body was healing at an astonishing rate and that he thought I was ready to take my first step. I was astounded! Even in my optimism, I assumed it would be at least six months to a year before I would be able to walk. However, that afternoon, I took my first step. Actually, I took three.

It took seven weeks of relearning to walk before I graduated from a wheelchair to a four-prong walking cane. I also regained vision in my left eye. I still didn't have use of my left hand, and doctors determined that I wasn't mentally capable of taking care of myself, so I was released into my parents' care. Although moving back in with Mom and Dad after I had been on my own for a couple of years wasn't my first choice, considering the circumstances, I was beyond grateful that they were able and willing to take care of me. Mom loved that I was moving back home!

Living with my parents and unable to work, I had a lot of time to think. I contemplated how I might be able to use my car accident to help others. When my youngest sister Amery died of heart failure at 18 months old, my parents had turned their pain into purpose and transformed our family's tragedy into leading support groups for other parents who had lost children. In addition, they orga-nized fundraisers for the hospital that attempted to save Amery's life. Their example inspired me to consider how I might do some-thing similar.

One day my dad was driving me to physical therapy when I reas-sured him that everything happens for a reason, but it's our respon-sibility to choose the reason. I told him, "Dad, do you remember how, before the accident, I was telling you that I love speaking at Cutco events and I want to be a professional speaker?" He nodded. He knew that I had been listening to professional speakers like Jim Rohn and Tony Robbins and that I wanted to help people the way that they did. "Well, until the accident, I never really had anything worth giving a speech about. I mean, you and Mom were great par-ents, and I've had a pretty normal life up until this point. But maybe that's why this happened to me—so that I can overcome my adver-sity and then teach people how to overcome their own."

Coincidence or not, my first opportunity presented itself just a few months later when I was invited to share my story with the stu-dents and faculty at my alma mater, Yosemite High School, which I'd graduated from just two years prior. Students were inspired, and I understood firsthand why my parents chose to turn their adversity into opportunities to help others. It was my turn to do the same.

My intent in sharing my story is to give you a real-life exam-ple of what can be overcome and accomplished, and how you can transform your adversities into opportunities, no matter what your life is like right now. Consider that anything another human being has done is evidence of what's possible for you. *You are just as worthy, deserving, and capable of creating anything you want for your life as any other person on earth.* I encourage you to read that sentence again (seriously) and deeply consider that it is as inher-ently true for you as it is for anyone else. And it is true no matter what your past or current circumstances might lead you to believe because what you're capable of—your potential—is truly limitless. This book will give you a critical tool to access more of your potential on a daily basis.

Grab a Pen

Before you read any further, please take a few moments to grab a pen or pencil so you can write in this book. As you read, mark anything that stands out that you may want to come back to later. Underline, circle, highlight, fold the corners of pages, and take notes in the margins so you can come back and quickly recall the most important lessons, ideas, and strategies. Set yourself up so that this book is a resource you can come back to again and again.

Are you ready?

Okay, with your pen in hand, let's get started! The next chapter of your life is about to begin.

IT'S TIME TO WAKE UP TO YOUR FULL POTENTIAL

"'Life's too short' is repeated often enough to be a cliché, but this time it's true. You don't have enough time to be both unhappy and mediocre. It's not just pointless; it's painful."
—**Seth Godin**

"Your past is not your potential. In any hour you can choose to liberate your future."
—**Marilyn Ferguson**

Why is it that when a baby is born, we often refer to them as "the miracle of life" and consider their potential to be limitless, but then we go on to accept mediocrity in our own lives? Where along the way do we lose sight of the miracle that *we* are living?

When you were born, everyone assured you that you could do, have, and be anything you wanted when you grew up. So, now that you're grown up, are you doing, having, and being anything and everything you've ever wanted? Or somewhere along the way, did you redefine "anything and everything" to include settling for less than you truly want and are capable of?

I once read an alarming statistic: the average American is more than 20 pounds overweight, more than $10,000 in debt, lonely, and disengaged at work, and has less than one close friend. I couldn't help but wonder why this becomes the reality for so many. And, more importantly, what do we do about it, so that we completely defy this statistic?

In 2020, all our lives were turned upside down by the COVID-19 pandemic. For many, the resulting mental health challenges became worse than ever. Others lost their source of income and ability to provide for themselves and their families. In the years that have followed, our collective uncertainty about the future seems to be at an all-time high. The problem is that when we focus on things that are out of our control, we feel out of control, which can cause us to experience stress, fear, anxiety, and even depression. At the end of the day (and the beginning), the only thing we can control is ourselves—what we do, who we become, and how we choose to show up for others. I would argue that becoming the best version of ourselves and creating the life we want is what we should be focused on each day.

What about you? Are you dedicating time to fulfilling your limitless potential and creating the level of success that you truly desire and deserve—in *every* area of your life? Or are there aspects of your life in which you're settling for less than you really want because you're overwhelmed with daily responsibilities, afraid of doing things differently, in need of economic security, or not sure how to make significant and lasting changes? Are you settling for less than you're capable of and then justifying why that's okay? Or are you ready to stop settling, and create a life that is so fulfilling you can't wait to wake up every day and live it?

Creating Your Level 10 Life

One of my favorite sentiments ever shared by Oprah was "The biggest adventure you can ever take is to live the life of your dreams." I couldn't agree more. Sadly, so few people ever come close to living the life of their dreams that the phrase itself has become cliché. Most people resign themselves to a life of mediocrity, passively accepting whatever life gives them. Even achievers who are highly successful in one area, such as business, tend to settle for mediocrity in another area, such as their health or relationships.

At the same time, human beings have an innate drive and desire for life to be as good as it possibly can be. We aspire to be as happy, healthy, wealthy, and successful as we can be, and to experience as much love, freedom, and fulfillment as possible. If we were to measure success and fulfillment on a scale of 1 to 10, I think it's fair to say that all of us would love to live each area of our lives at level 10. The problem is that few people are dedicating time each day to becoming the level 10 person they need to be—the person who is capable of creating and sustaining that life. I believe a commitment to daily personal development may be our greatest opportunity as individuals and collectively as a society.

What you're about to find out is that achieving this kind of level 10 success is not only possible but simple—the result of establishing a daily ritual that gives you purposeful time each day to evolve into the level 10 version of yourself.

What if I told you that it all starts with how you wake up in the morning and that there are small, simple steps you can start taking today that will enable you to become the person you need to be to achieve and maintain the levels of success you truly want and deserve—in *every* area of your life? Would you get excited? Would you even believe me? Some won't. Many people have become jaded, and rightfully so. They've tried everything under the sun to improve their lives and their relationships, and they're still not where they want to be. I understand. I've been there myself. Then, over time, I learned a few things that changed everything. I'm offering you my hand and inviting you to the other side, the side where life is not just better but also extraordinary in ways you may have only imagined it could be.

This Book Builds Upon Three Fundamental Truths

1. You are just as worthy, deserving, and capable of creating and sustaining extraordinary health, wealth, happiness, love, and success in your life as any other person on earth. It is imperative—not only for the quality of your life but also the impact you make on your family, friends, clients, coworkers, children, community, and anyone whose life you touch—that you start living in alignment with that truth.

2. To stop settling for less than you want—in any area of your life—and experience the levels of personal, professional, and financial success you desire, you must first dedicate time each day to becoming the person you need to be, who is capable of consistently creating those levels of success.

3. How you approach waking up each day and your morning routine (or lack thereof) is crucial because it sets the tone, context, and direction for the rest of your day. Focused, productive, successful mornings set you for focused, productive, successful days, which ultimately lead to an extraordinary life. The opposite is also true: unfocused, unproductive, and mediocre mornings pave the way for unfocused, unproductive, and mediocre days, culminating in an unfulfilled potential and a life of continuous struggle.

But Hal, I Am NOT a "Morning Person"

What if you've already tried waking up earlier, and it hasn't worked? "I'm just not a morning person," you say. Or "I'm a night owl" or "There's not enough time in the day" or "Besides, I need *more* sleep, not less!"

That was all true for me, too, before I created the Miracle Morning. In fact, it's true for most people. I've consistently surveyed hundreds of thousands of members of the global Miracle Morning Community, and I've always asked the following question: *Were you a morning person before you read* The Miracle Morning? Consistently, between 70 and 75 percent of our community of early risers confirm that they were *not* morning people before they read the book that you're now reading. Most of them identified as night owls. So, this is kind of a "welcome to the club" scenario.

Regardless of your past experiences, even if you've had trouble waking up early and getting going in the morning for your entire life, things are about to change.

The Miracle Morning is not only simple but also extremely enjoyable, something you'll soon be able to do easily and for the rest of your life. And, while you can still sleep in any time you want, you might be surprised to find you no longer want to. I can't tell you how many people have told me that they now wake up early—even on the weekends—simply because they feel better and get more done when they do. Imagine that.

In later chapters, I'll introduce you to the Life S.A.V.E.R.S., the engine that drives your Miracle Morning. This simple, memorable acronym comprises six of the most effective, timeless, and proven habits for personal development. After implementing these six habits, you'll be able to choose which ones to keep using and in which order to create your own customized Miracle Morning.

Because the Miracle Morning is customizable, it works with anyone's lifestyle. Even if you have an unusual schedule or unpredictable demands on your time, such as a newborn baby who wakes you up in the middle of the night or a job that requires you to work inconsistent hours, you can tailor your Miracle Morning to work with your schedule. I'll help you make it work in "Chapter 8: Customizing Your Miracle Morning."

You'll also be able to choose your wake-up time. There is no specific time that is required for this to work. Rather, the ideal wake-up time is whatever works best for your schedule. The point is to dedicate the first 6 to 60 minutes of your day to your Miracle Morning ritual so that you can develop the ability to create *your* level 10 life, however you define it.

Here are some common benefits people experience in some of the most important areas of life, which I encourage you to keep in mind as you go through this book. The more aware and intentional you are about these benefits, the more likely you are to experience them.

- **Happiness.** Each morning spent in solitude increases your awareness that your happiness is not dependent on outside forces (unless you allow it to be). Happiness is determined by your chosen perspective, as I illustrated in the introduction. Thus, you can *choose* to be happy each day, no matter how difficult your current circumstances are.

- **Health.** Whatever areas of life you focus your S.A.V.E.R.S. on is where you'll inevitably see improvements. So, if you focus on improving your health or fitness, losing weight, or increasing your energy, that's what you'll experience. I used my Miracle Morning to help me beat a rare form of cancer, and others have used it to lose weight, run marathons, overcome other health challenges, and otherwise optimize their health.

- **Relationships.** The Miracle Morning has improved countless relationships and even saved marriages for couples who were on the brink of divorce. When we become more intentional about who we're being and how we're committed to showing up for others, we gain the power to transform our relationships.

- **Finances.** As you'll learn in the next chapter, the Miracle Morning enabled me to avoid bankruptcy and more than double my income at the height of the worst economic recession in decades. By focusing your S.A.V.E.R.S. on increasing your income, you will be able to do exactly that.

- **Productivity.** Starting each day in a peak physical, mental, emotional, and spiritual state increases your ability to be more productive and stay focused on your top priorities. This is another way that your Miracle Morning will help you change your life, because it enables you to be more productive so that you can make those changes.

- **Leadership.** As you elevate your consciousness and become a better version of yourself, making meaningful improvements in your life, you inevitably inspire those around you and show them what's possible. You not only lead by example, you also become more capable of helping others follow your lead.

- **Confidence.** When you realize that *you* are in control of how you show up every day—and that's really one of the only things you are in control of—and start showing up at your best, you gain confidence.

I realize that these are bold claims to make, and this list of benefits might come across as overpromising—a little too good to be true, right? I assure you, there is no hyperbole here. The Miracle Morning is going to give you uninterrupted time each day to learn, grow, and become the person you need to be to achieve your most important goals and dreams (especially those you've been putting off).

Whether you currently consider yourself to be a morning person or not, you're about to learn how to make waking up every day easier and more enjoyable than it's ever been before. Then, by taking advantage of the undeniable relationship between early rising and extraordinary success, you'll find that how you begin your day becomes the key to unlocking your full potential and establishing the levels of success you desire in any area. You'll quickly see that when you change the way you wake up in the morning, you can change your entire life.

2

THE MIRACLE MORNING ORIGIN

Born Out of Desperation

"Desperation is the raw material of drastic change. Only those who can leave behind everything they have ever believed in can hope to escape."
—William S. Burroughs

"To make profound changes in your life, you need either inspiration or desperation."
—Tony Robbins

As much as we prefer for life to be easy and enjoyable, our greatest opportunities for growth are often masked by misfortune. It is on the other side of seemingly insurmountable circumstances, rising from the depths of despair, that we emerge as a better version of ourselves.

I've been fortunate to hit what you might call "rock bottom" twice in my relatively short life. I say *fortunate* because it was the growth I experienced and the lessons I learned during the most difficult times in my life that have enabled me to become the person I've needed to be to create the life I've always wanted. I am grateful to be able to use not only my successes, but also my failures, to help others in a way that can empower them to overcome their own limitations and achieve more than they ever thought possible.

The Miracle Morning didn't come to me as I was relaxing on a beach drinking mimosas (that certainly would have been much easier and more enjoyable). Instead, it emerged out of true desperation when I was enduring one of the lowest points in my life. Perhaps this is why it has resonated so powerfully with millions of readers.

My First Rock Bottom: Dead at the Scene

I consider my first rock bottom to be when I was hit by a drunk driver, a story I shared in the introduction. I woke up from a coma to face a much harsher reality than I could have ever conceived, and I was very fortunate to have an abundance of love, support, and encouragement from other people during that time. In the hospital, someone was always there to take care of me. I was constantly surrounded by my loved ones as family and friends came by daily to check on me. I had an incredible staff of doctors and nurses overseeing every step of my care and recovery. I didn't have the everyday stresses of work and bills. My only responsibility was to heal, and even that I had help with. Although my recovery was painful and certainly not without its challenges, I felt completely supported and life in the hospital was relatively easy.

My Second Rock Bottom: Deep in Debt and Deeply Depressed

My second rock bottom took place in 2008 at the height of the Great Recession. The economy had crashed, and I had crashed along with it. Like millions of Americans, I was experiencing my own personal financial crisis. Seemingly overnight, my successful small business was no longer profitable. My clients were suffering from the effects of the recession and couldn't afford to pay me for coaching. In a matter of months, my income dropped by more than half. I was suddenly unable to pay my bills and began living on credit cards. I had recently bought my first home and now I couldn't afford the mortgage. I was engaged to be married, and we were planning our first child. Drowning in debt and behind on my mortgage, for the first time in my life I became deeply depressed. I experienced a complete mental, emotional, and financial breakdown.

Why Debt Was Worse Than Death

If you were to ask me which was more difficult, my car accident or my financial crisis, I wouldn't hesitate to tell you it was the latter, by far. Most people would probably assume that being hit head-on by a drunk driver, breaking 11 bones, suffering permanent brain damage, and waking from a coma to be told that you may never walk again would be harder to overcome than relatively common financial struggles. It's a fair assumption. However, this wasn't the case for me.

Not being able to pay my bills, watching my business fail, going deeper and deeper into debt, and having my house seized by the bank were new experiences that I wasn't mentally or emotionally equipped to handle. The abundance of love and support that I had while I was recovering from my car accident was nowhere to be found. Nobody felt sorry for me. I didn't have any visitors. There was no one there to oversee my care and recovery. I was on my own. People had their own problems to deal with.

Feeling alone made this time of my life much worse. Yes, I had emotional support from Ursula, and she did her best to encourage me, but she couldn't solve my financial problems. She couldn't fix the economy, let alone my business. Every day was a struggle. I was consumed with so much fear and uncertainty that the only comfort I found was retreating to the safe haven of my bed each night. It offered temporary relief as I could escape having to face my problems for seven or eight hours. But, of course, my problems were there waiting for me when I woke up.

I had never felt so hopeless, and the thought of committing suicide plagued my mind daily. I contemplated how I might do it in a way that would create the least amount of pain for the people I loved. Looking back, it feels like an overreaction. But at that time, I felt helpless and afraid, and I desperately wanted to end the emotional pain I was experiencing. However, considering how much taking my life would devastate my parents was enough for me to suck it up and keep moving forward.

Deep down, I always believed that no matter how bad things get, there is *always* a way to turn it around. But the thoughts and feelings were still there. I just didn't see a way out of my financial crisis, and I hated feeling so incapable.

The Run That Changed My Life

Not wanting to burden anyone with my problems, and probably a little embarrassed that I couldn't handle my responsibilities, I kept all of this to myself. That is, until Ursula suggested it was time to swallow my pride and reach out to one of my friends to ask for help.

I called my longtime friend Jon Berghoff, who had been exceptionally successful in business and was known for being wise beyond his years. I felt a sense of relief as I finally confessed how badly I was struggling. I held nothing back. And while he expressed his genuine concern, his initial advice caught me off guard. He asked me if I was exercising every day.

Feeling confused by his question, I responded with, "What does exercising have to do with me not being able to pay my bills?"

"A lot."

Jon went on to explain that whenever he was feeling stressed or overwhelmed, going for a run enabled him to think more clearly, lifted his spirits, and helped him come up with solutions to his problems. I immediately objected, "Jon, I hate running. What else can I do?" Without hesitation, he retorted, "What do you hate worse, running . . . or your current circumstances?"

Ouch. Touché. All right. I was desperate. I had nothing to lose. So, I decided to go for a run.

The next morning, I laced up my Nike Air Jordan basketball shoes (I'm telling you, I wasn't a runner), grabbed my iPod so I could listen to something positive that I hoped would improve my mindset, and headed out the front door of my soon-to-be-bank-owned home. I had no idea that, on my very first run, I would hear a quote that would change the course of my entire life.

I was listening to a personal development audio from Jim Rohn, and he said something that, although I had heard it before,

I had never really understood or applied it. You know how sometimes you have to hear something at the right time for it to finally click? That morning I was in the right state of mind—a state of desperation—and I got it. When I heard Jim proclaim with certainty, "Your level of success will seldom exceed your level of personal development because success is something you attract by the person you become," I stopped in my tracks.

I rewound the audio and replayed that line again. *Your level of success will seldom exceed your level of personal development because success is something you attract by the person you become.* It was like a tidal wave of reality came crashing down, and I suddenly became present to the fact that I had not been dedicating time to developing myself into the person I needed to be to attract, create, and sustain the levels of success that I wanted in my life. On a scale of 1 to 10, I wanted to experience level 10 success, but my level of personal development was hovering at around a two—maybe a three or a four on a good day.

It suddenly made sense. While my problems and the causes of my depression appeared to be external—a failing business, not enough money to pay my bills, having my home foreclosed on, the state of the economy, and so on—the solution was internal. If I wanted to live a level 10 life, I needed to first become a level 10 person who could create that life.

Over the years, I've realized that this is the disconnect for most people. We all want to experience each aspect of our lives—health, happiness, relationships, spirituality, financial security, you name it—as close to a level 10 as possible. No one *wants* to settle for less. But only a relatively small percentage of the population has a daily personal development practice that enables them to continuously evolve into the person they need to be to create that life. Back then, I definitely didn't have one. What I needed was to start dedicating time to my personal development, each day, so that I could become capable and deserving of the life I wanted.

Feeling inspired and hopeful for the first time in a long time, I turned around and ran back to my house. I was ready to become the person I needed to be to transform my life.

The First Challenge: Finding Time

It made sense to me that making personal development a priority in my daily life was the solution to most of my problems—the missing link that would enable me to evolve into the person I needed to be able to change my life. Simple enough.

However, my first hurdle was the same as it would be for anyone else: *finding the time*. As important as I knew this was, I didn't know how I was going to fit one more thing into my packed schedule. I already felt so busy and overwhelmed, just trying to make it through the day, that the idea of finding "extra" time for my personal development seemed like it would add more unwanted stress to my life. Maybe you can relate?

This brought to mind something I had read in Matthew Kelly's book, *The Rhythm of Life*: "On the one hand, we all want to be happy. On the other hand, we all know the things that make us happy. But we don't do those things. Why? Simple. We are too busy. Too busy doing what? Too busy trying to be happy."

I grabbed my planner, sat down on my couch, and committed to finding the time—*making* the time—to start incorporating a daily personal development ritual into my life. I considered my options.

Maybe the Evening?
My first thought was that I could find time in the evening, either directly after work or late at night after Ursula went to bed. But I quickly realized that evenings were the only time we spent together during the week. Not to mention, after a long day of work I was

usually mentally and physically drained. I just wanted to relax. I was hardly coherent, let alone in an optimal state of mind to engage in personal development. The evening was not going to be an effective time.

Possibly the Afternoon?

Next, I considered the afternoon. Maybe I could schedule it in the middle of the day, possibly on my lunch break. Or maybe I could find some extra time somewhere in the middle of my never-ending to-do list. But it just wasn't realistic. The afternoon was not going to work, either.

Aw, Come On . . . NOT the Morning!

Finally, I contemplated doing it in the morning. Immediately, I resisted. To say that I was *not* a morning person was an understatement. I had always resisted the idea of waking up early. It was something I despised almost as much as I despised running. You would have never caught me running for the sake of running, just as you would have never caught me waking up early unless I had somewhere I needed to be. But the more I thought about it, the more a few things started to make too much sense to ignore.

I figured that if I started each day with a personal development ritual, I'd probably be in a much better state of mind for the rest of the day. I remembered a blog post that I'd read on StevePavlina.com titled "The Rudder of the Day." Steve compared the morning to the rudder on a ship: "If I'm lazy or haphazard in my actions during the first hour after I wake up, I tend to have a fairly lazy and unfocused day. But if I strive to make that first hour optimally productive, the rest of the day tends to follow suit."

Second, if I got my personal development done first thing in the morning, I could avoid all of the excuses that accumulate during the day (*I'm too tired, I don't have time, I'll do it tomorrow*, etc.). By carving out time in the morning, before the rest of my life and work got in the way, I could all but guarantee it would happen every single day.

The morning was clearly the best option. But it was hard enough to drag myself out of bed every day at 6 AM *when I had to*, so the idea of voluntarily waking up an hour earlier was borderline inconceivable to me. I was about to close my planner and forget the whole idea when I heard the distinct voice of one of my mentors, Kevin Bracy, passionately shouting in my head: "If you want your life to be different, you have to be willing to do something different first!"

Damn it. I knew Kevin was right. It was time to see if I could overcome my life-long, albeit self-imposed, limiting belief that I was not a "morning person." I wrote "Personal Development" into my schedule at 5 AM the next morning.

The Second Challenge: Doing What's Most Impactful

Then I encountered another challenge: What could I do for that hour to make the biggest impact and improve my life the fastest? I needed to figure out what highly successful people did for their personal development and then model it. I wanted to discover what the most effective practices and methods were so that I could get the most bang for my buck.

I grabbed my computer and googled phrases like "best personal development practices" and "what do the world's most successful people do for personal development?" I pulled out a piece of blank paper and began writing down what I discovered. What I found were all timeless practices. None of them were new. At first, I was disappointed. I had been conditioned by society to always be on the lookout for "new." We've all been trained by marketers to value the newest iPhone, the new season of our favorite show, and the latest, most cutting-edge, never-before-seen solutions to our problems. Simultaneously, we are taught to devalue things that are timeless, proven, and effective, which we mistakenly dismiss as old and out-dated. What my search was yielding were activities that weren't just old, they had been around for thousands of years. I ended up with a list of six practices: *meditation, affirmations, visualization, exercise, reading,* and *journaling.*

It occurred to me that what each of these practices had in common was that many, if not most, of the world's most successful people from all walks of life have credited one or more of them as being essential to their success. Each of these was time-tested and proven. It also occurred to me that I wasn't doing any of them consistently. But which one should I do? Which one was the best? Which of these practices would enable me to change my life the fastest?

Suddenly, I had an epiphany: *What if I were to wake up tomorrow, one hour earlier, and do all six practices?* I thought. *That would be the ultimate personal development ritual!* I quickly divided 60 minutes by 6 practices, assigned them 10 minutes each, and planned to try all six the next morning. The interesting thing was, looking at this list got me feeling motivated! All of a sudden, the idea of waking up early went from something I normally avoided to something I was actually looking forward to. That night, I fell asleep with a smile on my face. I was excited for the morning to come!

The Morning That Changed Everything

When the alarm clock sounded at 5 AM (which would have previously been an unthinkable time for me to wake up), my eyes shot open, and I sprang out of bed feeling energized and excited. It reminded me of being a kid on Christmas morning. There had been no time in my life when waking up had been easier and more enjoyable . . . until today.

Teeth brushed, face washed, and a glass of water in hand, I sat up straight on my living room couch at 5:07 AM, feeling genuinely excited about my life for the first time in a long time. It was still dark outside, and something about that felt very empowering. I pulled out my list of life-changing personal development activities, and one by one, I implemented each practice.

Meditation. I set a timer for 10 minutes, and I sat in silence, praying, meditating, and focusing on my breath. Initially, my mind was racing with thoughts. *Am I doing this right? How do I quiet my mind? Why can't I stop thinking?!* Although I initially felt frustrated with the chaos of my mind, as the minutes passed by, time seemed to slow down. Though I had never meditated before, and I was sure that I was doing it wrong, I felt my stress melting away and being replaced by a sense of peace. With each breath, my mind felt more at ease. This was radically different from the mental chaos and reactivity that I typically began each day with. For the first time in months, I felt *peaceful*.

Affirmations. The next activity was the one I was arguably the least excited about. Telling myself "I am wealthy" when I was anything but seemed to be delusional at best. However, during my search the night before, I had come across the self-confidence affirmations from Napoleon Hill's classic book *Think and Grow Rich*. These provided a simple reminder that we can all source our confidence from within based on the unlimited potential that is inside each of us. They affirmed that we are all inherently just as worthy, deserving, and capable of overcoming and accomplishing anything we desire as any other person on earth. Reading them aloud, I felt *empowered*.

Visualization. I figured that if many of the world's most elite athletes and performers used visualization to mentally rehearse performing at their best, there was no reason it couldn't help me to do the same. I found that closing my eyes and visualizing myself going through my day feeling focused, confident, and happy was as much about the feelings I generated as it was about what I pictured. I generated a compelling emotional experience that fueled my desire to take actions that were in alignment with what I visualized. I felt *inspired*.

Reading. Having always made excuses about why I didn't have time to read, I was excited to make time this morning and start what I had always hoped could become a lifelong habit. I grabbed *Think and Grow Rich* off the shelf again. Like most of my books, it was one that I had started but never finished. I read for 10 minutes and picked up a few ideas that immediately improved my mindset. I was reminded that it only takes one idea to change your life. I felt *motivated*.

Journaling. Next, I opened one of the many blank journals I had purchased over the years. Like all the others, I had only written in it for a few days—a week at the most. On this day, I wrote what I was grateful for in my life. I also penned a few possibilities for the future, optimistically expressing gratitude for the better life situation that I was committed to creating. Almost immediately, I felt my depression lifting like a heavy fog that had been weighing me down. It was still there, but it felt lighter. The simple act of writing down the things I was fortunate to have in my life but often took for granted lifted my spirits. I felt *grateful*.

Exercise. With 10 minutes left on the clock, I was ready to move my body and get the blood flowing. I stood up from the couch and did 60 jumping jacks. As out of shape as I was, that was enough to get me breathing heavy. Then, I dropped down on the living room carpet and did as many push-ups as I could (I'll keep that number to myself). Then I flipped over onto my back and did as many sit-ups as my out-of-shape abs could muster. With six minutes to go, I pressed play on a five-minute yoga video that I had found the night before on YouTube. Though I had a long way to go before I got back into shape, I felt *energized*.

Sixty minutes had gone by in a flash, and I felt incredible! I had experienced what was one of the most peaceful, empowering, inspiring, motivating, grateful, and energizing days of my life—and it was only 6 AM. I was hopeful. I thought, *If I start every day like this, it's only a matter of time before I become the person that I need to be to create everything I want for my life.*

When Ursula woke up, I couldn't wait to tell her how my morning went! I enthusiastically walked her though each step and expressed that I believed this morning ritual could be the one thing that changed everything for us. She was noticeably skeptical. "So wait, let me get this straight. You've been feeling depressed and hopeless for six months, and now, after just one morning, you are somehow feeling confident that you can turn things around. Are you on drugs?" she asked with a laugh.

"No, but I'm telling you, sweetheart, it feels like a miracle!"

Nothing Short of a Miracle

For the next few weeks, I continued to wake up at 5:00 AM and follow through with my new 60-minute personal development ritual. And I was so incredibly happy with the way I was feeling and the progress I was making as a result of my morning routine, I wanted *more* of it. So, one night while getting ready for bed, I did what was unthinkable at the time; I set my alarm clock for 4:00 AM. Falling asleep that night, I wondered if I was out of my mind. Surprisingly, it was just as easy to wake up at 4:00 AM as it was 5:00 AM, and waking up at either time was ten times easier than waking up on *any* day in the past.

My stress levels dropped dramatically. I had more energy, clarity, and focus. I felt genuinely happy, motivated, and inspired. Thoughts of depression were quickly becoming a distant memory. You could say I was back to my old self again, only I was experiencing so much growth, so rapidly, that I quickly surpassed any version of myself that I had ever been in the past. And with my newfound levels of energy, motivation, clarity, and focus, I was able to set goals, create strategies, and execute a plan to save my business, get more clients, and increase my income. In fact, less than two months after my first Miracle Morning, I had more than doubled my monthly earnings. Not only was my income back to the level it had been before it crashed, but it was higher than it had ever been before.

I found myself consistently reflecting on the transformation I was experiencing, how profound it was, and the speed at which it was happening. I told Ursula that it felt like a miracle, and she started calling it my "miracle morning." That resonated with me, so I changed "Personal Development" to "Miracle Morning" in my schedule. And I began to think about sharing my morning routine with others. I figured if this was working so well for me, even though

I wasn't a morning person when I started, then maybe it could help other people, too. So, I felt compelled to pay it forward. But before I got a chance to figure out how I was going to do that, someone took the initiative to ask me about it.

Hey, If Katie Can Do It . . .

A few weeks later, I was still working out how best to share what I'd discovered with others in a way that would be easy to replicate when my coaching client Katie Heaney brought up the topic of mornings herself. "Hal, I keep reading about successful people who swear by their morning routines. How do you start your mornings?" she asked. I could hardly contain my excitement as I told her all about my new Miracle Morning ritual and the benefits I was experiencing. Like I had, she immediately pushed back: "Yeah, that makes sense. But I just don't know that I want to wake up any earlier. I've just never been a morning person."

"Neither was I!" I assured her. I offered her some encouragement and gave her some tips on beating the snooze button. She committed to waking up at 6 AM, one hour earlier than her usual wake-up time, and giving the Miracle Morning a try.

On our next coaching call, two weeks later, Katie showed up with more enthusiasm than I'd ever heard from her! When I asked whether she woke up at 6 AM every day to do her Miracle Morning, I got an unexpected reply: "Nope. I woke up at 6 AM on the first day, but you were right—I had such an awesome morning that I wanted more of it! So, I woke up at 5 AM the rest of the week! Hal, it was amazing!"

I was so inspired by her experience that I immediately began sharing the Miracle Morning with all my other coaching clients. Like Katie, most of them were initially resistant to the idea, each proclaiming they weren't a morning person. However, with a little persistence and encouragement, and using Katie's example as evidence of what was possible, everyone committed to waking up at least 30 minutes earlier to implement the Miracle Morning.

Within a few short weeks, 13 out of 14 of my clients were doing the Miracle Morning and telling me that they were experiencing profound benefits similar to the ones that Katie and I had seen. Just the fact that they were meditating, reciting affirmations, visualizing, exercising, reading, and journaling every day was worth celebrating. Some of them started proudly telling their friends and coworkers that they were doing the Miracle Morning, and it was changing their life. A few began posting daily updates about it on social media. Suddenly, the idea began spreading, and I started to see strangers—people I had never met—posting about *their* Miracle Morning online.

Crazy, right?

Who the Heck Is Joe?

To help support people who were just discovering the Miracle Morning, a friend suggested that I buy the domain name Miracle Morning.com (I couldn't believe it was available!) and post some video blogs. I wasn't comfortable being on camera, but I decided to give it a shot. I started recording short videos, uploading them to YouTube, and putting them up on my new homemade website.

One morning, sitting on my living room couch, I was uploading one of my videos to YouTube when I typed my name into the search. (Hey, don't judge. You know you've googled yourself before.) A video popped up that was titled "Miracle Morning at Joe's." It was from some guy that I had never seen before in my life, and my first reaction was not very positive. I got defensive and said out loud, "Who the heck is Joe, and why is he copying my Miracle

Morning?!" I didn't know what to think. Boy, was I about to be pleasantly surprised.

I hit play on the video, and this is what I saw. "Hello, it's your friend, Joe Diosana. Let's look at the time." Joe showed his alarm clock, which read 5:41AM. "It is 5:41 in the morning—on a Sunday! And you must be wondering, 'Dude, Joe, what in the world are you doing up at 5:41 in the morning on a Sunday?' Well, check out MiracleMorning.com. Look at the information and download it. It feels like Christmas to me, honestly, and I've got a lot of energy. It's like Christmas every day now. Check it out, and I hope your life will be blessed."

I sat staring at my computer screen, my mouth hanging wide open. I was in awe and almost in tears. I was beginning to realize that, while I never intended for the Miracle Morning to be anything more than my own personal development ritual, I now felt a sense of responsibility to share it with as many people as possible, so that it could impact their lives the way it had mine.

It was becoming clear that if the Miracle Morning worked for me, Katie, Joe, and nearly everyone I had shared it with—and none of us considered ourselves to be morning people—it could work for anyone.

How Will You Use the Miracle Morning?

I've spent a fair amount of time in this chapter explaining how the Miracle Morning came to be and telling you how the practice has enhanced other people's lives. Now that you have a better understanding of what's possible, it's time to shift the focus toward how the Miracle Morning can enhance *your* life.

The following chapters are about taking yourself to the next level so you can take your success to the next level. Remember, it only happens in that order. By making consistent daily progress toward becoming a level 10 version of yourself, you can create the level 10 life you truly want and deserve.

I won't ask you to sleep any less, nor will I harp on you to get up an hour earlier. Remember, the Miracle Morning is completely customizable to fit your lifestyle. Many people do a 30-minute Miracle Morning (roughly five minutes for each practice), and it can be done in as little as six minutes, total (see "Chapter 7: The 6-Minute Miracle Morning"). You'll also see that there are other times of the day when you can implement this if mornings simply do not work for you.

I would ask that you start to consider the risks versus the benefits. Is settling for less than you truly want in *any* area of your life worth hitting the snooze button for those extra 30 minutes of sleep in the morning? Or would creating everything you want for your life be worth waking up a little bit earlier? Don't answer that question yet. Just keep it in mind as you read the next chapter.

3

THE 95% REALITY CHECK

"One of the saddest things in life is to get to the end and look back in regret, knowing that you could have been, done, and had so much more."
—Robin Sharma

"The story of the human race is the story of men and women selling themselves short."
—Abraham Maslow

Every day, you and I wake up and face the same universal challenge: overcoming the temptation to settle for less than we're capable of so that we can live to our full potential. It's arguably the greatest challenge in nearly every person's life—to rise above the gravitational-like pull toward mediocrity and to show up at our best each day so that we can create a life that we absolutely love waking up to.

According to the Social Security Administration, if you take any one hundred people at the start of their working careers and follow them for the next 40 years until they reach retirement age, you'll find that only one will be wealthy, four will be financially secure, five will continue working—not because they want to, but because they have to in order to pay their bills—36 will be dead, and 54 will be broke and dependent on their friends, family, and the government to take care of them.

Only 5 percent of the population succeed in creating a life of freedom, monetarily speaking. Everyone else, the other 95 percent, will struggle their entire lives. And while of course money is by no means the only—or even the best—measure of success, it can certainly represent safety, comfort, contribution, and freedom. When we're financially secure, we are free to stop worrying about money and focus on the other areas of our life that matter most.

When I created and began practicing the Miracle Morning, my financial situation was such a mess. So, I focused my practice on increasing my income. Even though America was in the middle of the 2008 Great Recession, I was able to more than double my income in less than two months by doubling the number of clients I worked with. As I began to get my finances in order, I began focusing on my health and fitness (which had been steadily declining, since being depressed made it difficult for me to get motivated). I changed my diet and committed to running an ultramarathon (since that's what I decided would represent level 10 fitness for me). My mental health also completely transformed, though that didn't take two months. It literally shifted during my very first Miracle Morning as I went from feeling hopeless to hopeful. And, of course, Ursula loved seeing this new and improved me, which transformed our relationship. It is clear to me that when you focus on improving yourself in any area, every area of your life improves as a result.

With this awareness, there is one crucial question that I believe we must explore and find answers to: What can we do now to stop settling for less than we're capable of so that we can create the level 10 life we deserve to live?

Three Steps to Rise Above Mediocrity and Fulfill Your Potential

I've found that the word *mediocrity* can be triggering for some people. If you were to interpret it as a judgment, or condescending in some way, you might receive it as an insult, which is understandable. However, that is certainly not my intention nor the intended meaning, so I'll take a moment to clearly define the term as it is used throughout this book.

Mediocrity has nothing to do with how you or I compare to any other person. It is simply a matter of how we compare to the person we are capable of being—the best version of ourselves. When we settle for less than we want and are capable of, we are settling for mediocrity as it relates to the potential that is within us.

When researchers from Cornell University asked thousands of people on their deathbeds to name the biggest regret in their entire life, 76 percent of participants had the same answer: "Not fulfilling my ideal self." I don't know about you, but I find it disheartening to think that three-quarters of the population will reach the end of their life and look back with regret, thinking, *I wish I'd had the courage to fulfill my potential and live the life I was capable of living.*

We don't need statistics to tell us that most people are struggling to create a life they love. We can look around at the people in our circle of influence, at society as a whole, or at the person staring back at us in the mirror and make our own assessment. How many people do you know who are living or even attempting to live life at a level 10? On the flip side, how many people do you know who are settling for less than they want and struggling to enjoy life?

The rest of this chapter lays out three simple, decisive steps to rise above mediocrity and join those who are living life on their terms.

Step 1: Acknowledge the 95% Reality Check

First, we must understand and acknowledge the sobering reality that 95 percent of society may never create and live the life they really want. Of course, our friends and family are not immune to this fate, and neither are we. It's simply a matter of cause and effect. So, it's crucial to embrace the perspective that if we don't commit to thinking and living differently than most people, we may be unintentionally setting ourselves up to endure a life of struggle—like most people. If we want to fulfill our potential and help those we love to do the same, we must make different choices, starting now.

It is human nature to take the easy path, despite the consequences. Since we can't control what other people do, we must focus on ourselves. In doing so, we can better position ourselves to help others. It's kind of like when the flight attendant tells you in the event of an emergency, put your oxygen mask on first. When we prioritize our self-care, we are better equipped to help others.

Every day, most of us struggle with some important aspect of our lives. We struggle to create the levels of success, happiness, love, fulfillment, health, and financial prosperity that we truly desire. Consider the following:

- **Physically.** Obesity is an epidemic. Potentially fatal conditions like cancer and heart disease continue to plague our society. The average person reports being exhausted, and most of us struggle to generate enough energy to make it through a single day without consuming a few cups of coffee or an energy drink. Yet, despite being exhausted during the day, our minds tend to race in the evening, and millions of people struggle to get a good night's sleep. Our physical energy level is crucial to our quality of life. When we have an abundance of energy, we feel happier, more motivated, and more capable, and thus we are able to be more productive. On the flip side, when we're fatigued, exhausted, or in pain, we usually feel more depressed, motivation is harder to come by, and we feel incapable of being productive, let alone making major changes in our lives. Something has to change.
- **Mentally and emotionally.** We all want to feel good. We want to be happy. We want to enjoy life. Yet more and more of us are struggling to find joy and meaning in our lives. A recent poll shows that only 14 percent of American adults say they're "very happy." According to Mental Health America (MHA), 46 percent of Americans will meet the criteria for a diagnosable mental health condition sometime in their life, and half of those people will develop conditions by the age of 14.
- **Relationally.** The quality of our lives is largely influenced by the quality of our relationships, and sadly, more people than ever describe feeling lonely, isolated, and disconnected from their friends and family. Roughly half

of all marriages still end in divorce. Many couples who stand before their friends and family and commit their lives to each other—*through the good times and the bad*—struggle to uphold their vows. As a society, many would agree that we have become more divided than ever. We are longing for connection.

- **Financially.** Americans have more personal debt today than at any other time in history. Few people are earning as much money as they'd like to be. Most of us spend more than we make, don't save enough, and struggle to pay the bills, let alone create financial freedom.

If you were to ask anyone who is unhappy, unfulfilled, or struggling in significant ways whether their current situation was part of their life plan, what do you think they would say? Do you think anyone intends for their life to be a struggle? Of course not! And that is the scary part, because people are allowing life to happen to them rather than actively creating the life they want.

Now that we've acknowledged that a majority of our society is not living the life that they envisioned, the next crucial step is to understand *why*—to help you avoid the same fate, or to find your way out if you are already in this group.

Step 2: Identify the Causes of Mediocrity and the Solutions

We will spend most of our time in this chapter on this second step because identifying what's standing between who we are and who we are capable of being is crucial to closing that gap. Let's explore seven common causes of mediocrity, accompanied by seven solutions you can immediately implement to overcome them. Consider which of these you can relate to and then simply begin applying the corresponding solutions.

Cause 1: Rearview Mirror Syndrome

One of the most crippling causes of unfulfilled potential is a perspective that I call rearview mirror syndrome (RMS). Our subconscious minds are equipped with a self-limiting rearview mirror through which we continuously relive and re-create our past. We mistakenly believe that who we *were* is who we *are*, thus limiting our true potential in the present based on limitations we may have accepted for ourselves in the past.

As a result, we filter every choice we make—from what time we wake up to which goals we set to what we allow ourselves to consider possible—through the limitations of our past experiences. We want to create a better life, but it's difficult to see ourselves any other way than how we've always been.

On any given day, the average person thinks between 50,000 and 60,000 thoughts. The problem is that the majority of our thoughts are the same, or very similar, from one day to the next. This causes us to develop thought patterns. We habitually think the same thoughts and generate the same feelings and moods, day after day. Self-doubt becomes a thought pattern. Fear becomes a thought pattern. Anger becomes a thought pattern. This continues until we make a conscious decision and sustained effort to elevate our thinking. It's no wonder most people go through life, day after day, month after month, year after year, and struggle to improve the quality of their lives.

Like old, worn baggage that needs to be replaced, we carry stress, fear, and worry from yesterday with us into today. When presented with new opportunities, we quickly check our rearview mirror to assess our past capabilities: "Nope, I've never done anything like that before. I've never achieved at that level. In fact, I've failed, time and time again." Similarly, when faced with adversity, we go back to our trusty rearview mirror for guidance on how to respond: "Yep, just my luck. This crap always happens to me. I'm just going to give up; that's what I've always done when things get too difficult."

Solution 1: Embrace Your Limitless Potential

To expand beyond the limitations of your past, you must stop perceiving your worth and capabilities through your psychological rearview mirror. You must be willing to see what's possible for you through the lens of your inherent limitless potential. You can start by embracing and affirming the paradigm "What I'm capable of is based on my potential, not my past."

The Miracle Morning practice will provide a framework to upgrade your habitual, unconscious thought patterns and program your subconscious mind to experience and produce more of what you want in your life. You'll be able to develop the confidence that, regardless of your past, you are capable of creating what you want for your life, from now on.

This may be counterintuitive, but it's not even necessary to believe it at first. In fact, you probably won't believe it. You may find that trying to establish the belief that you can be better than you've been in the past feels uncomfortable and inauthentic. That's to be expected. But soon you'll be able to replace the struggles and limitations of your past with inspiring options and opportunities for your future.

Cause 2: Lack of Purpose

If you ask the average person what their life purpose is, you might get a funny look or a response along the lines of, "Geez, I don't know. I'm just trying to make it through the day." What if I asked you? What would you say?

Our life purpose is the underlying "why" that compels us to wake up each morning and do everything in our power to achieve what we want in life. People who know their life purpose have a heightened level of clarity that enables them to take decisive action each day. However, most of us were never taught how to identify our life purpose, so understandably, most people don't have one.

Though our purpose might be one of the most important considerations of our lives, the concept may not have been introduced to us by our parents and certainly isn't addressed in most schools. Instead, we usually find ourselves focused on just trying to get through another day, taking the path of least resistance, and pursuing short-term, short-lived pleasures while avoiding any pain or discomfort that would enable us to grow and evolve.

If you want to fulfill your true potential, getting clear on your life purpose can make all the difference. Having a clearly defined life purpose means having set goals and a direction for one's life. It will essentially serve as both the engine and navigation system that drive your thoughts and actions throughout your days. Your purpose will streamline your decision-making and help consistently move you in the right direction.

Solution 2: Choose a Life Purpose

Now, I get that coming up with your "life purpose" may feel a little intimidating, but I have good news: You don't have to figure it out. Instead, you get to make it up. *And* you can change it any time you want. Your purpose can be any chosen way of being and/or serving others that inspires you to wake up every day and live in alignment with the person you want to become. It could be a general way of being/serving, such as "become the best version of myself and help others do the same" or "enjoy every moment of this one life I've been blessed to live and be a source of joy for others." It could also be more specific, such as "providing financial security for my family" or "getting clean drinking water to millions of people." There are no wrong answers here.

Your life purpose need not be grandiose. Not every purpose needs to end with "and change the world." Your purpose is intended to inspire and bring out the best in *you* every day, not necessarily change the world. Yet it's those who make the choice to identify and live in alignment with their purpose that typically make the biggest impact for others.

Your life purpose can and will likely change or evolve over time. As you continue to grow and evolve, so, too, will your purpose. What you choose today is not set in stone. Knowing that you are not committing to one single defined purpose for the rest of your life may make settling on something now easier. I like to think that choosing a life purpose is like trying on and buying clothing. See how it fits and how it makes you feel, wear it for as long as it serves you, and be open to making changes when appropriate. Here are examples of different life purposes that I've adopted over the years:

- *Be the most positive person I know.* (age 19)
- *Selflessly add value to the lives of every person I possibly can.* (age 25)
- *Become the person I need to be to create everything I want for my life while helping others do the same.* (age 29)
- *Help to elevate the consciousness of humanity, one person at a time, beginning with elevating my own consciousness.* (age 42)

You may notice that all these life purpose statements are either about becoming a better version of myself or helping others do the same.

Personally, I believe that the greatest gift we can give to another person is fulfilling our potential so that we can show them what's possible, lead by example, and help them fulfill theirs. I imagine that if every person was striving to live to their full potential and helping others do the same, we'd have a society of people who were much happier, fulfilled, and productive. But that's just me. Your purpose can be about being the parent your kids deserve or achieving financial freedom. Again, there are no wrong answers.

Cause 3: Isolating Incidents

One of the most prevalent but not-so-obvious causes of mediocrity is the concept of isolating incidents. This happens when we mistakenly assume that each choice we make, and each individual action we take, only affects that specific moment or circumstance. For example, we may think it's no big deal to miss a workout, procrastinate on a project, or eat fast food because we'll get a do-over tomorrow. We make the mistake of thinking that skipping that workout only impacts us on that day, and we'll make a better choice next time. But when we do this, we're missing the bigger picture.

The real impact and consequence of each of our choices and actions—and even our thoughts—is monumental because every single thought, choice, and action is determining who we are becoming, which will ultimately determine the quality of our lives. As T. Harv Eker said in his bestselling book *Secrets of the Millionaire Mind*, "How you do anything is how you do everything."

Every time you choose to do the *easy* thing (anything that is out of alignment with your values or with achieving your goals), instead of the *right* thing (anything that is in alignment with your values and will move you closer to your goals), you are shaping your identity into someone who does what's easy instead of what's right. On the other hand, when you choose to follow through with your commitments—especially when you don't *feel* like it—you are developing the extraordinary discipline necessary for creating extraordinary results in your life (which, unfortunately, most people never choose to develop).

Solution 3: Be Present to the Impact of Your Choices

We must stop isolating incidents like this in our minds and start seeing the bigger picture. Realize that every choice you make impacts who you're becoming, which is determining the life you're capable of creating. When you're present to this perspective, you take the alarm clock more seriously. When the buzzer goes off in the morning and you're tempted to hit the snooze button, you start thinking, *Wait, this is not who I want to become—someone who doesn't even have enough discipline to get out of bed in the morning. I'm getting up now because I am committed to _____ (waking up early, achieving my goals, becoming the person I need to be to create everything I want for my life, etc.).*

Consider that who you're becoming is far more important than what you're doing and that it's what you're doing that is determining who you're becoming.

Cause 4: Lack of Accountability

Accountability is the act of being responsible to someone else for some action or result, and the link between accountability and achievement is irrefutable. Consider that most highly successful people, from executives and CEOs to professional athletes and top performers from all walks of life, embrace a high degree of accountability. It gives them the leverage they need to take action and produce extraordinary results, particularly when they don't feel like showing up at their best. Accountability brings out the best in people.

Consider also that most of the positive results you and I produced from birth to about age 18 were thanks to the accountability provided for us by the adults in our lives (parents, teachers, bosses, etc.). Vegetables were eaten, homework was completed, teeth were brushed, we bathed, and we got to bed at a reasonable hour. If it weren't for the accountability provided for us by these adults, we would have been malnourished, uneducated, sleep-deprived, dirty little kids.

Think back to an occasion when you knew someone was counting on you to meet them somewhere, but you didn't feel like going. Maybe it was for a workout at the gym or for a dinner out, and if it weren't for them expecting you to show up, you would have just stayed home. Aren't we always more likely to show up and follow through when we have someone else we're accountable to?

The reality is that accountability has brought order to our lives and allowed us to progress, improve, and achieve results we wouldn't have otherwise. The problem is that most of us tend to resist or altogether reject accountability. We do so because it was never something we asked for. Rather, it was forced on us by adults against our will. No kid ever said, "Hey Mom, will you do me a favor and hold me accountable to brushing my teeth and maintaining other positive habits in my life? Thanks."

As with most things forced upon us, we grew to resent accountability. Then, when we turned 18, we embraced every ounce of freedom we could get our hands on, continuing to avoid accountability like it was the plague. This attitude toward accountability is largely responsible for perpetuating our downward spiral into settling for mediocrity, causing us to develop detrimental mindsets and habits, such as being lazy, procrastinating, deflecting responsibility, and generally doing the minimum amount required to get by. Of course, all of this is counterproductive to fulfilling our limitless potential.

Take this book, for example. The reality is that most people who read any nonfiction book never implement what they learn because no one is holding them accountable to do so. I'm guessing you might be able to relate to this yourself. Have you ever finished reading a book, one that contained life-changing information, and the only action you took was choosing the next book you were going to read? Yeah, me too. There is a way to change that.

Solution 4: Re-establish Accountability in Your Life

Now that we are all grown up and striving to achieve success and fulfillment, we must invite accountability back into our lives. To do this, take responsibility for initiating your own strategy for accountability (or moving back in with your parents). Your account-ability strategy could be as simple as reaching out to a friend, family member, or coworker—anyone who might support you in follow-ing through with your commitments—and inviting them to be your accountability partner. Or, if you want to take it up a notch and work with someone who is trained in the skill of effectively holding people accountable, you can hire a professional coach.

To leverage the power of accountability in your life, and spe-cifically to help support you in implementing your new Miracle Morning ritual, I recommend that you take a few minutes to con-sider who you could ask to be your accountability partner. I'm sug-gesting you do this now, while you're reading this book, so that by the time you get to "Chapter 10: The Miracle Morning 30-Day Life Transformation Journey," you have someone that you can receive support and encouragement from while providing the same. Both of you will benefit from holding each other accountable to follow-ing through.

If you're thinking, *No one I know would do this with me*, consider that you really don't know where someone is at mentally and emo-tionally, what they're dealing with internally, and whether they're ready (or desperate) for change.

If you're more comfortable in a group setting, as opposed to one-on-one, you can also form a small accountability group made up of multiple people. I've done this by inviting a handful of my colleagues to a weekly group call to hold each other accountable and support one another in reaching our individual goals. The result was that all five of us measurably had the best year in our careers.

If you don't have someone in mind, or you're convinced that no one you know would be up for being your accountability partner, you're always welcome to request an accountability partner online in the Miracle Morning Community. This is quite common in the community. To quickly and easily reach out for an accountability partner, post something simple and straightforward like: "I just started reading *The Miracle Morning*, and I'm looking for an accountability partner to support each other in doing the 30-Day Journey. I'm in the central time zone, so please let me know if you're up for it. Thanks!" Keep in mind that anyone who responds to this is likely the type of person you want to have in your circle of influence!

To be clear, in no way is it required that you have an accountability partner to start your Miracle Morning 30-Day Journey. I didn't have one when I started mine. However, re-establishing consistent accountability in your life can be one of the most effective ways to get out of your comfort zone and take your results (in any area) to the next level. So, I'd urge you to commit 10 to 15 minutes to making a list of potential accountability partners, and consider inviting them to join you on your Miracle Morning journey.

Cause 5: Mediocre Circle of Influence

There's that word again: mediocre. Remember the context: being mediocre is defined as *settling for less than you want and are capable of*—something we all struggle with. With that said, I think we often underestimate the importance of the company we keep, unaware of the impact that our circle of influence is having on our mental health, quality of life, and levels of success in nearly every aspect of our lives. Let's take a few moments to thoughtfully consider this.

Jim Rohn famously stated, "You are the average of the five people you spend the most time with." While this principle is sound, I think the number is somewhat arbitrary. For example, if you spend most of your time with only one person, that individual's way of thinking, their emotional state, and their habits will affect you—influencing the way you think, your emotional state, and your habits.

If the people you spend the most time with are generally happy and emotionally intelligent, then you are likely to become happier and more emotionally intelligent just by being in their presence. If the members of your inner circle all value eating healthy foods, you aren't likely to show up at a get-together holding a bag of McDonald's. And if you spend time with people who earn substantial incomes and are good with money—even if you enter their circle earning far less—their way of thinking and earning money will surely rub off on you and help you increase your level of financial success.

On the contrary, if the people you spend most of your time with are generally unhappy, unhealthy, emotionally unstable, struggling financially, constantly complaining, and consistently settling for mediocrity (less than they're capable of), it will influence you to do all the above. If the people you associate with are not striving to improve their lives, then they're not going to challenge or inspire you to do any better.

Solution 5: Upgrade Your Circle of Influence

Being intentional and proactive about seeking out like-minded people, those who share your values and are on a similar path, is one of the most effective ways to improve your life. Unfortunately, many readers are ready to improve themselves and their lives but are surrounded by people who aren't striving to improve anything. This can be especially challenging when those people are your family or your significant other.

Although you can't control what anyone else does, you can control what you do. Ultimately, you must decide whom you're committed to being (positive, successful, happy, courageous, generous, etc.) and how you are going to live your life, no matter whom those closest to you may choose to be and how they choose to live. In other words, upgrading your circle of influence begins with upgrading yourself. In the same way that the people you spend time with influence your way of thinking and being, how you show up influences the people around you.

As you practice your Miracle Mornings and start to elevate your consciousness—becoming more aware and intentional about how your thoughts, words, and actions impact you and those around you—you will naturally notice and be attracted to people who operate at a similar level of consciousness. These people usually don't fall into your lap, though. You must actively seek out people who are like-minded and will contribute to your personal evolution. Find people who are positive and proactive, who believe in you, who will support and encourage you, and who improve the quality of your life just by being around them.

It is often said that "misery loves company," but so does mediocrity. Don't let the fears, insecurities, and limiting beliefs of others limit what's possible for you. One of the most important commitments you will ever make is proactively and continuously improving your circle of influence. Always seek people who will add value to your life and bring out the best in you. And of course, be that person for others.

Cause 6: Lack of Personal Development

While all human beings were born with an innate drive and desire to fulfill our potential and create the most meaningful life possible, most of us aren't investing time each day toward consistently developing the qualities and characteristics that will enable us to create that life. As a result, we find ourselves unintentionally submitting to an ongoing struggle to attain the levels of health, happiness, love, confidence, financial security, and success that we truly desire.

Consider that when you fail to make time for personal development, you may be forced to endure unwanted suffering. Remember Jim Rohn's philosophy that inspired me to create the Miracle Morning in the first place: "Your levels of success will rarely exceed your level of personal development, because success is something you attract by the person you become." In a sense, this is the essence of the Miracle Morning—turning personal development into a daily practice.

Solution 6: Develop a Daily Personal Development Ritual

Personal development is the practice of self-improvement. Your level of personal development is a general assessment of your current mindset, knowledge, skills, beliefs, habits, and so on. Establishing and committing to a daily personal development ritual will enable you to continuously learn, grow, and evolve into the person you need to be to both create the life you want and enjoy the life you have.

A better life is available to you no matter what's happened in your past because a better you is available. The key to that life is developing the mindset, capabilities, and habits you need to consistently create and live that life. The Miracle Morning is a daily ritual that ensures you make time for personal development so that you can continually develop yourself into the person you are striving to become. As you get better, life gets better.

Cause 7: Lack of Urgency

The underlying cause of unfulfilled potential—which prevents people from making any significant improvements to their quality of life—is that we have no inherent sense of urgency to do anything differently. Unless we're facing an emergency, human nature is to put things off as long as possible.

We tend to live with a "someday" mindset and mistakenly assume that life will either work itself out (if you're an optimist) or that there's no point in even trying (if you're a pessimist). Either way, this someday mindset is perpetual, and it leads to a life of procrastination, unfulfilled potential, and regret. Someday is never today, and so our time to make meaningful changes never comes. Lacking urgency, we may find ourselves waking up one day and wondering what the heck happened. How did our life end up *like this*? How did *we* end up like this?

Solution 7: Make Every Day the Most Important Day of Your Life

We've all experienced the pain of regret, as a result of thinking and talking ourselves into being, doing, and having less than we are capable of. Mediocre days turn into mediocre weeks. Mediocre weeks turn into mediocre months. Mediocre months inevitably turn into mediocre years.

We must now embrace the perspective that *today* matters more than any other time in our lives, because it's what we choose to do each and every day that determines who we're becoming and what we'll be capable of doing tomorrow. If we make good choices today, we'll be more capable of making good choices tomorrow.

On the other hand, if you don't make the commitment *today* to develop yourself into the person you need to be to create the level 10 life that you and your loved ones deserve, what makes you think tomorrow, next week, next month, or next year are going to be any different? They likely won't. That is why you must consciously choose to maintain a sense of urgency to make every day count.

Step 3: It's Time to Draw Your Line in the Sand

In this chapter, we've identified seven causes of mediocrity and how you can overcome them. We've acknowledged the reality that society has conditioned us to settle for less than we are capable of. You're well aware that most people struggle to create the life they want and that, if you and I don't commit to thinking and living differently than most people, there's a very good chance that we, too, will inevitably end up settling and struggling.

This third and vital step to rising above mediocrity is to *draw your line in the sand* by deciding what you are going to start doing differently from this day forward. Not tomorrow or next week or next month or someday. Your entire life changes the day that you decide you are no longer willing to settle for less than you are capable of. If you haven't done this already, let *today* be that day for you—the day you decide that today is the most important day of your life because who you are becoming, based on the choices you make and the actions you take, is determining who you are going to be for the rest of your life.

Whether or not you realize it, you are already elevating your consciousness by becoming more aware and intentional about how your thoughts, words, and actions impact you and those around you. Thus, you are already on your path toward becoming the person you need to be to create and live the life you deserve.

So, let us take the next step in this exciting journey by considering an important question . . .

WHY DID YOU GET OUT OF BED THIS MORNING?

"You've got to get up every morning with determination if you're going to go to bed with satisfaction."
—George Lorimer

"Your first ritual that you do during the day is the highest leveraged ritual, by far, because it has the effect of setting your mind, and setting the context, for the rest of your day."
—Eben Pagan

W hy did you bother getting out of bed this morning? Think about that for a second. Why do you wake up at the time you do, most mornings? Why do you leave the comfort of your warm, cozy bed? Is it because you *want* to? Or is it because you *have* to?

If you're like most people, you wake up to the incessant beeping of an alarm clock each morning and reluctantly drag yourself out of bed because you have to be somewhere, do something, answer to or take care of someone else. We hit the snooze button and resist the inevitable act of waking up, unaware that our resistance is sending disempowering messages to our subconscious mind, such as "I don't have enough discipline to get out of bed, let alone do what I need to do to change my life."

If given the choice between staying in bed for as long as possible or getting out of bed to start the day in an optimal way (because it doesn't usually feel like we have a choice), most people would rather stay in bed.

You Snooze, You Lose: The Truth About Waking Up

The old saying "you snooze, you lose" may have a deeper meaning than any of us realized. When we resist waking up and delay getting out of bed, we're simultaneously resisting our opportunity to wake up and create the life we claim that we want. When we respond to the sound of the alarm clock with an internal dialogue along the lines of, "Oh no, it's morning already. I have to wake up. I don't want to wake up," we're also telling ourselves (and the universe, if you believe in that sort of thing), "I know I *say* that I want to improve myself and my life, but not as much as I want to lay here, unconscious, for a little bit longer." Consider the kind of suboptimal mindset we are embodying when we begin our day with this resistance.

Repeatedly pressing the snooze button also has an unavoidable physiological impact. According to Robert S. Rosenberg, medical director of the Sleep Disorders Center of Prescott Valley in Flagstaff, Arizona, "When you hit the snooze button repeatedly, you're doing two negative things to yourself. First, you're fragmenting what little extra sleep you're getting, so it is of poor quality. Second, you're starting to put yourself through a new sleep cycle that you aren't giving yourself enough time to finish. This can result in persistent grogginess throughout the day."

Many people who struggle to get out of bed when the alarm sounds report that the morning is the most difficult time of day for them. They wake up feeling stressed about some aspect of their life or life in general, so they delay waking up and getting out of bed for as long as possible. For some people, it is because of a job they feel obligated to go to or due to a relationship that is failing. Some people feel this way due to chronic depression and its ability to weigh on a person's mind, emotions, and heart without being able to name a specific reason.

Regardless of the cause, failing to start our morning with intention and purpose can have a detrimental impact on our mental health and emotional well-being. It becomes a vicious cycle: we wake up with despair, spend the day ruminating over stressful thoughts and emotions, lay down to bed feeling anxious or depressed, then repeat the cycle of melancholy the next day.

Conversely, when you have a morning personal development ritual in place, one that ensures you start each day with intention, purpose, and self-optimization, you interrupt the cycle. Instead of going to bed feeling stressed and worried about waking up to face your problems, you can now go to bed each night feeling hopeful and excited about starting your day with proven practices to improve your life. Having a morning ritual acts as a kind of buffer against dealing with life's challenges. Rather than waking up and immediately feeling stressed and overwhelmed, you begin each day in an optimal mental, physical, emotional, and spiritual state, which will enable you to manage difficult circumstances, enjoy life, and achieve your goals more effectively.

How Much Sleep Do We Really Need?

In the first edition of *The Miracle Morning*, I failed to emphasize the importance of getting adequate sleep. I kind of glossed over it. But sleep is one of the most consequential tools for optimizing our mental, physical, and emotional health. We will delve much deeper into this topic in "Chapter 11: The Miracle Evening," but I think it's important to begin addressing it here.

When it comes to how many hours of sleep we need to perform at our best, sleep experts will tell you that there is no universal number that applies to everyone. National Sleep Foundation guidelines advise that healthy adults need between seven and nine hours of sleep per night. Babies, young children, and teens need even more sleep to enable their growth and development. People over 65 should also get seven to eight hours per night.

The optimal number for you is influenced by variables such as age, genetics, overall health, exercise (or lack thereof), diet, stress level, and evening rituals (including how close to bedtime you eat your last meal), just to name a few. While you may be at your absolute best sleeping six to seven hours, someone else may find that they function optimally on eight or nine hours.

Since age and genetics are out of our control, I find it much more useful to focus on the factors that we can control—namely diet, exercise, and our evening rituals. For example, if your diet consists of processed foods, preservatives, artificial flavors and dyes, pesticides, and excessive sugar and carbohydrates, then your body may require more sleep to deal with the detrimental effects of such foods and to eliminate any toxins that you've consumed. Similarly, if you eat too close to bedtime (within an hour or two), you are burdening the body with digesting your food while you're trying to sleep instead of giving it uninterrupted time to purely rest and rejuvenate.

On the other hand, if you eat a diet primarily consisting of healthy, nutrient-dense whole foods—such as organic fruits, vegetables, and meats—and you finish your last meal a few hours before bedtime (giving your body time to properly digest your final meal of the day), then your body will be able to rest and rejuvenate much more easily. The person who eats a healthy diet will almost always have more energy and function more optimally, even with less sleep, than the person who eats poorly.

Since there is such a wide variety of opposing evidence from countless studies and experts, and since the amount of sleep needed varies from person to person, I'm not going to attempt to make a case that there is one *right* approach to sleep. Instead, I'll share my own results, from personal experience and experimentation and from studying the sleep habits of some of the greatest minds in history. I'll warn you: some of this may be somewhat controversial.

How to Wake Up Feeling More Energized

Through experimenting with various sleep durations, I discovered something quite unexpected: how we feel in the morning is largely affected by our own personal *belief* about the amount of sleep we need and how we're going to feel in the morning. In other words—and this is an important distinction—how we feel when we wake up is based not only on how many hours of sleep we get, but also on how much sleep we believe we need and how we tell ourselves we're going to feel in the morning.

For example, if you believe that you need eight hours of sleep to feel rested but you're getting into bed at midnight and have to wake up at 6 AM, you're likely to tell yourself, "I'm only getting six hours of sleep so I'm going to feel exhausted in the morning." Then, what happens as soon as your alarm clock goes off and you realize it's time to wake up? What's the first thought that enters your consciousness? It's typically the same thought that you had before bed: "Just as I thought; I only got six hours of sleep, and I feel exhausted." It's a self-fulfilling, self-sabotaging prophecy. If you tell yourself you're going to feel tired in the morning, regardless of how many hours of sleep you get, then you are setting yourself up to feel tired. If you believe that you need eight hours to feel rested, then you're not going to feel rested on anything less. But what if you changed your beliefs?

Developing a basic understanding of what's often referred to as the mind-body connection (or what scientists call the "biopsychosocial paradigm") has become increasingly useful as research continues to prove that our thoughts, feelings, beliefs, and attitudes can positively or negatively affect our biological functioning. The brain and body are connected through neural pathways, and communication occurs via chemical and physical messengers, such as neurotransmitters and hormones. These messengers transmit signals between the body and the brain to control our everyday functions, from breathing, digestion, and pain sensations to heart rate, thinking, and emotions. This means that your thoughts and emotions are actually physical processes, and they have a meaningful effect on the systems in your body. However, you don't need a scientific study to tell you that when you go to bed feeling stressed and overwhelmed, you typically wake up feeling stressed and overwhelmed.

Personally, I've had multiple firsthand experiences that have shown me the physiological power we wield when we consciously and intentionally use our mind-body connection. Remember that, after my car accident, doctors said I would never walk again. However, I chose to believe that I could. I meditated and visualized my body healing and saw myself walking. I affirmed, with unwavering faith and optimism, that I would walk again. And three weeks after my car accident, after breaking my leg and pelvis in multiple places, my doctors were baffled when a routine X-ray showed that my body had healed beyond what they believed to be possible. Later that day, I took my first step. That prompted me to begin studying the mind-body connection so I could better understand and apply it.

A few years ago, I had the opportunity to interview famed cancer surgeon and bestselling author Dr. Bernie Siegel. He said that of the thousands of cancer patients he treated over his 40-plus-year career, the one thing that nearly all survivors had in common was their mindset and, specifically, their belief in their ability to heal. He said that he worked with many patients who, statistically, should *not* have survived, and the one thing they had in common was that they maintained an unwavering belief that they were going to survive, even though the odds were stacked against them. He said that he also saw countless patients—those with far less deadly cancers—give up the belief that they were going to heal and sadly not make it.

Based on scientific research, the countless experiences of other people, and my own experience, I reckon that if we can use our minds to defy the odds and overcome seemingly insurmountable physical ailments, then we can use that same mind to influence the quality of our sleep and how we feel in the morning. To test this theory, I have experimented with various sleep durations—from as little as four hours to as many as nine. The only other variable in my experimentation was the intention I set about how I was going to feel in the morning based on the number of hours I slept. First, I told myself, right before bed, that I was *not* getting enough sleep and that I was going to feel exhausted when I woke up in the morning. Entertaining this belief before bed became a self-fulfilling prophecy.

On four hours of sleep, I woke up feeling exhausted.

On five hours of sleep, I woke up feeling exhausted.

On six hours of sleep, you guessed it—I felt exhausted.

Seven hours, eight hours, nine hours—the hours of sleep I got didn't significantly change how I felt when the alarm clock went off in the morning. As long as I told myself that I wasn't getting enough sleep and that I was going to feel tired in the morning, that's exactly how I felt.

Then, I conducted the same experiment with a different intention. I recited the following empowering bedtime affirmation to wake up feeling energized and excited in the morning, no matter how many hours of sleep I got:

I am grateful that I'm getting ___ hours of sleep tonight. My mind and body are capable of extraordinary things, the least of which is generating an abundance of energy from ___ hours of sleep. I know that my mindset influences my biology, so I choose to wake up tomorrow feeling energized and excited to do my Miracle Morning.

Whether I got nine, eight, seven, six, five, or as little four hours of sleep, as long as I consciously decided before bed that I was getting enough sleep and that I was going to wake up feeling energized, I consistently woke feeling better than I ever had before. However, don't take my word for it. I encourage you to experiment with this yourself.

To be crystal clear, I am not suggesting that telling yourself you're getting enough sleep trumps the importance of getting enough sleep. Adequate, consistent sleep is crucial to your brain's and body's ability to function optimally, and sleep deprivation can be devastating to your physical, mental, and emotional well-being. What I am suggesting is that what you tell yourself before bed impacts how you feel in the morning. So, you must take responsibility for setting yourself up for success at bedtime so that you can wake up each morning feeling energized and excited, regardless of how many hours of sleep you get.

So, how many hours of sleep do you *really* need? You tell me.

We will talk more about setting up a bedtime ritual to help you optimize your sleep in "Chapter 11: The Miracle Evening." And if you'd like to delve even deeper into learning how to optimize your sleep, I recommend reading *Sleep Smarter: 21 Proven Tips to Sleep Your Way to a Better Body, Better Health, and Bigger Success* by Shawn Stevenson. It's a favorite of mine, and one of the most well-researched books on the topic of sleep.

The Secret to Making Every Morning Feel Like Christmas

Think back to a time in your life when you couldn't wait to wake up in the morning. Maybe it was to catch an early flight for a vacation that you'd been anticipating for months. Maybe it was growing up, looking forward to your first day of school. Or your first day at a new job. Maybe it was your wedding day or your birthday. Personally, I was never more excited and energized to wake up in the morning—regardless of how many hours of sleep I got—than when I was a kid on Christmas morning. Maybe you can relate?

Whatever those occasions were for you, how did you feel when those mornings arrived? Did you have to drag yourself out of bed? Doubtful. On mornings like these, we can't wait to wake up! We do so feeling energized and genuinely excited. We quickly toss the covers off and spring to our feet, ready to take on the day! Imagine if this is what *every day* of your life is like. It can be.

The Miracle Morning is largely about recreating the experience of waking up feeling energized and excited, and doing so every day of your life, for the rest of your life! It's simply a matter of taking a few minutes to set your intention before bed and consciously decide how you are going to feel when you wake up in the morning. It's about starting your day with purpose—not because you *have* to but because you genuinely *want* to—and dedicating time to developing yourself into the person you need to be to create the most extraordinary, fulfilling, and abundant life you can imagine.

But wait—for those of us who spent most of our lives believing that we are *not* morning people, there may be one final obstacle to us waking up excited every day, ready to jump out of bed and create the lives we want. Which obstacle am I speaking of? It is the almost irresistible temptation of . . . *the snooze button.*

THE 5-STEP SNOOZE-PROOF WAKE-UP STRATEGY

"If you really think about it, hitting the snooze button in the morning doesn't even make sense. It's like saying 'I hate getting up in the morning, so I do it over, and over, and over again.'"
—Demetri Martin

"I'd like mornings better if they started later."
—Unknown

H i, *my name is Hal, and I am a recovering snooze-aholic. It's been 15 years, 3 months, and 12 days since my last snooze.* All kidding aside, if it weren't for the simple five-step strategy you're going to learn in this chapter, I would still be addicted to the habit of repeatedly hitting the snooze button and adhering to my lifelong, self-limiting belief that I was not a "morning person." Let's talk about how to overcome both of those.

I've heard it said that nobody really likes having to wake up early, but everyone loves the feeling of having woken up early. The same is often said about exercising—that nobody really likes working out, but everyone loves the feeling of having gotten in a workout.

Although thinking that we're not going to enjoy a new habit may be true in the beginning, once the habit is established and we've experienced the benefits, it not only becomes automatic and enjoyable but also can become difficult *not* to do. For example, my wife struggled to start working out again after a long layoff, and now she loves going to the gym and is disappointed when she can't. Personally, I love waking up in the morning and doing my S.A.V.E.R.S., as do most Miracle Morning practitioners. It's become so ingrained, and is still so beneficial to my quality of life, that it's difficult *not* to do.

One perspective that helped me, as I began waking up earlier, was that I was merely trading unproductive evening time for highly productive morning time. Suddenly, instead of staying up late watching TV, scrolling social media, drinking alcohol, or engaging in otherwise mind-numbing activities, I was trimming the fat at the end of my day so I could reap the benefits of productive mornings. Your Miracle Mornings do not require any compromise to your sleep—that time can be sourced from the biggest time wasters in your day.

Increasing Your Wake-Up Motivation Level

Consider your average morning. The moment your alarm clock sounds, if you were to rate your level of motivation as it pertains to waking up and getting out of bed on a scale of 1 to 10 (10 being ready to wake up and start your day, and 1 meaning you want nothing more than to go back to sleep), where would you rate yourself? That number is what I call your wake-up motivation level (WUML), and I think it's safe to say that most of us would probably rate ours closer to a 1 or a 2 than a 10. It's perfectly natural when you're still half-asleep to want to hit the snooze button and keep on sleeping. That's the effect of sleep inertia.

The question is, how can you generate the motivation you need to get out of bed and create an extraordinary start to the day when your WUML is only at a 1 or 2 the moment your alarm clock starts beeping?

The answer is *one step at a time.*

The Five-Step Snooze-Proof Wake-Up Strategy

Here are five simple snooze-proof steps that make waking up in the morning and beating the snooze button easier than ever before.

Step 1: Set an Empowering Intention Before Bed

The first step to set yourself up for a successful morning is to remember this: *Your first thought in the morning is typically whatever the last thought was that you had before you fell asleep.* The same is true for your mental and emotional state. If you go to bed thinking stressful thoughts and feeling worried or overwhelmed, you'll likely wake up thinking and feeling the same. Whatever mental and emotional state you dwell on at bedtime weighs on your subconscious mind while you sleep and affects how you feel when you wake up. So, it only makes sense that we prioritize being highly intentional about what we think about and dwell on as we're drifting off to sleep.

The first step to waking up in an optimal mental and emotional state is to take responsibility for and be proactive about waking up in an optimal mental and emotional state. The easiest way to do that is to consciously set an empowering intention, right before you lay down to fall asleep, for how you're going to feel when you wake up. We'll be exploring bedtime affirmations, as well as other tools for ending your day best prepared for the Miracle Morning, in Chapter 11.

This first step—setting an empowering intention before bed—is more impactful than you might realize and should not be overlooked. Remember, your mental and emotional state in the morning is typically whatever mental and emotional state you dwelled on as you fell asleep. This can't be overstated. In just a few minutes each night, you can set an empowering intention to wake up feeling energized and excited to optimize your day.

Step 2: Move Your Alarm Clock Across the Room

This may be one of the easiest and yet most effective strategies for getting yourself out of bed in the morning. Simply move your alarm clock as far away from where you sleep as possible. I keep mine on my bathroom sink. This ensures that you get out of bed the moment the alarm sounds and that you immediately move your body. Movement generates energy, so when you get up and walk over to turn off your alarm clock, it naturally helps you to feel more awake so that you can stay awake.

Here's another way to look at it: every minute you are awake and upright, your wake-up motivation level increases. Simply setting yourself up so that you have to get out of bed and walk across the room to turn off the alarm clock will instantly take your WUML from a 1 to a 2 or a 3. However, you still might not feel ready to start your day. So . . .

Step 3: Brush Your Teeth

I know, I know. You're probably thinking, *Hal, seriously, did you just tell me to "brush my teeth"? Are you suggesting that oral hygiene is the solution to this whole struggle to get going in the morning?* Not exactly. The point here is giving yourself some mindless activities that keep your body in motion and give you more time to continue waking up.

After turning off your alarm clock, go directly to the bathroom sink and simply brush your teeth. While you're at it, you might splash some warm (or cold) water on your face. This simple activity will give you more time to acclimate to the day and continue increasing your wake-up motivation level from a 2 or a 3 to a 3 or a 4. Now that your mouth is minty fresh and you're starting to feel more awake, it's time to rehydrate.

Step 4: Drink a Full Glass of Water

You may or may not realize it, but after six to eight hours without water, we are mildly dehydrated when we wake up, and dehydration causes fatigue. When people feel tired—at any time of the day—what they often need is more water, not more sleep.

You're not hydrating while you're unconscious, and it is well documented that we lose as much as a liter of fluid during sleep through perspiring and expelling water vapor every time we exhale. Thus, it is imperative that you make it a priority to begin rehydrating as soon as possible after waking up.

For many people, coffee is their morning beverage of choice. And while coffee has many benefits, rehydrating isn't one of them. Coffee is a diuretic and can cause further dehydration. Don't worry, you can absolutely have your morning latte; I just wouldn't recommend doing so until you've consumed at least one glass of water.

For added benefits, including replenishing as many as 84 essential minerals and electrolytes, increasing your energy, detoxifying your liver, and even helping you lose weight (since research shows that staying hydrated helps the body increase its metabolism), simply add a pinch of Himalayan sea salt and fresh lemon juice into your water. This concoction also provides vitamin C, boosts immunity, and helps you feel rejuvenated inside and out.

To help me remember to drink water first thing in the morning, I place a glass of water on my bedside table just before I head to bed. After brushing my teeth in the morning, I immediately drink about half of it, then I begin sipping the rest.

The objective here is to rehydrate your body and mind as quickly as possible to make up for the water that you did not get during the hours you slept. When you drink a glass of water and hydrate yourself, your wake-up motivation level continues rising from a 3 or a 4 to a 5 or a 6.

Step 5: Get Dressed in Your Workout Clothes

Finally, get dressed in whatever clothing you prefer to exercise in, so you're ready to leave your bedroom and immediately engage in your Miracle Morning practice, which will incorporate a brief period of exercise (the *E* in S.A.V.E.R.S.). These extra few minutes of mindlessly getting dressed not only give your mind and body more time to wake up, increasing your WUML to a 6 or a 7, but also send a clear message to both your subconscious and your conscious mind that you are officially up for the day.

It only takes a few minutes to execute each of these steps, and when you do, your WUML naturally increases, making it much easier to stay awake and generate the energy needed to do your Miracle Morning. Attempting to make that decision when your alarm clock sounds and your WUML is still hovering around a 1 is much more difficult.

Miracle Morning Community Bonus Wake-Up Tips

Keep in mind that although this simple five-step strategy has proven to work for countless people, these five steps are not the only way to make waking up in the morning easier. One major benefit of being part of the global Miracle Morning Community is that each person is focused on optimizing their rituals and routines, sharing what's working, and actively supporting the community. Here are a few tips I've seen shared by members of the Miracle Morning Community:

- **Use a vibrating alarm clock.** If you sleep next to someone who is adversely affected by the sound of an alarm clock going off in the morning, such as a spouse or a baby, you may need to get creative to keep in that person's good graces. Luckily, there are dozens of options for vibrating alarm clocks. There are two primary designs: wearable technology, such as a wristwatch, and a vibrating pod that goes under your pillow. Just go to Google or Amazon and search "vibrating alarm clock" to see your options.
- **Set a timer for your bedroom heater.** If you struggle to get out of bed in the morning because it's uncomfortably cold where you live, this tip may be useful. One member of the Miracle Morning Community said that in the winter, she keeps a portable heater next to her bed, plugged into an appliance timer that is set to turn on 15 minutes before her alarm clock sounds. That way when she wakes up, the room is warm, and she isn't as tempted to crawl back

under her covers to avoid the cold. She said it makes a huge difference!

- **Keep caffeine next to the bed.** I hesitated to include this tip in the updated and expanded edition of this book because it runs somewhat counter to what I wrote earlier about starting your day with coffee, but hear me out. Something I've been doing recently is making a packet of Pique organic jasmine green tea (it's finely ground powder that easily mixes with room-temperature water) and keeping it on my bedside table. It only requires a minimal six to eight ounces of water and provides 45 to 55 grams of caffeine. Green tea is loaded with polyphenols that have remarkable health benefits, as well as the amino acid L-theanine, which helps balance the effects of caffeine. Studies have shown it to help increase focus and attention, too. As soon as my alarm clock sounds, I drink the entire glass of green tea in one shot, so that while I'm following the rest of the snooze-proof wake-up steps, the caffeine is kicking in to increase energy and mental clarity. I'll take all the help I can get! Of course, I immediately follow this by drinking a full glass of water to rehydrate.

Feel free to customize your own snooze-proof wake-up strategy. Remember, the objective is having a simple, effective, predetermined step-by-step process that requires minimal effort and makes waking up and getting going as easy as possible.

Don't wait to implement this! Start *tonight* by moving your alarm clock across the room, setting an empowering intention before bed, placing a glass of water on your nightstand to drink after you brush your teeth, and then getting dressed in your workout clothes so that you're ready to engage in the S.A.V.E.R.S., which the following chapter will cover in detail.

6

THE LIFE S.A.V.E.R.S.

6 Habits That Will Transform Your Life

"Success is something you attract by the person you become."
—Jim Rohn

"An extraordinary life is all about daily, continuous improvements in the areas that matter most."
—Robin Sharma

S tressed. *Worried. Overwhelmed. Frustrated. Unfulfilled. Blah.* These are a few unpleasant words that provide a rather unfortunate but fairly accurate description of how the average person far too often feels about his or her life.

Of course, life can be difficult. Our circumstances can feel unfair. Most of us have endured our share of challenges, and not everyone is fortunate enough to be born into a supportive environment. We haven't all had the same opportunities. However, every single one of us was born with the unlimited potential to become the best version of ourselves. What that looks like for you is different from what it looks like for me or for anyone else, but who we are becoming is the one thing we have control over and where we should invest our time and energy.

Although we can't go back in time and change the past (so there's no point wasting time and energy wishing we could), we can absolutely begin making meaningful changes to fulfill our potential, starting now.

The Potential Gap

Have you ever felt like you were living on the wrong side of a gap between who you are and who you could become? Like the life you want to live and the person you need to be to create that life are just beyond your grasp? When you see people who are achieving levels of success that you're not, do you ever feel like they've got it all figured out—like they must know something that you don't, because if you knew *it too*, then you'd be enjoying the same levels of success?

Most of us live on the wrong side of a gap that separates who we are from the person we could become. We are often frustrated with our lack of consistent motivation, effort, and results. We spend too much time *thinking* about the actions we should be taking to create the results that we want, but then we don't take those actions. Most of us *know* what we need to do; we just don't consistently *do* what we know. Can you relate?

This potential gap varies in size from person to person. You may feel like you're doing almost everything in your power to maximize your abilities and that a few tweaks could make all the difference. Or you might feel the opposite—like you've been living so far below your potential that you don't even know where to start. Whatever the case is for you—whether you are sitting on the wrong side of the Grand Canyon of your potential and wondering how you're going to get to the other side, or you've been working your way across the canyon but are stuck at a plateau and haven't been able to get to the next level—this chapter will introduce you to six habits that will enable you to close that gap.

It's Time to Save the Life You Deserve to Live

When I set out to determine what the single most effective personal development practice was, the one that would change my life the fastest, I couldn't narrow it down to just one. In fact, I ended up with a list of six: meditation, affirmations, visualization, exercise, reading, and journaling. And my epiphany came when I considered how powerful it could be if I combined all six of them.

A few months into writing this book, I was feeling frustrated that I didn't have a coherent, memorable way to connect, organize, and present these practices. One day, I took a break from writing and went looking for Ursula to ask for her perspective. I expressed my frustration, and she immediately responded with a potential solution (like she usually does). "Why don't you use a thesaurus and see if you can find synonyms for some of the words, and try to create an acronym to connect the six practices and make it easy to remember?" I loved the idea, told her she was brilliant, gave her a kiss, and went back to my computer. Soon, *meditation* became *silence*, *journaling* became *scribing*, and the following emerged:

- Silence
- Affirmations
- Visualization
- Exercise
- Reading
- Scribing

I wrote down "Life S.A.V.E.R.S." and got excited because the acronym felt very authentic and appropriate—these six practices *had* literally saved me from missing out on being able to create the life I aspired to live. While none of the items on this list were new to me and are likely not new to you, these are six of the most timeless, proven personal development practices, which many of the world's most successful people, across all walks of life, have sworn by for centuries. Consistently practicing any *one* of these can elevate your consciousness and help you become a better version of yourself. When you combine all six, you are harnessing the benefits of *all* of these ancient best practices to accelerate your personal development and transformation.

When you consider the words *meditation*, *affirmations*, and *visualization*, some preconceived notions may come to mind, and some of them may be negative. Often, these timeless rituals have been popularized in inadequate and even silly ways. For example, affirming something that isn't true, such as "I am a millionaire" or even "I am happy," when you're anything but, can feel inauthentic and like a waste of time. So, any negative preconceptions you may have are reasonable. But I encourage you to be patient and open-minded as you read this chapter. You'll find that each of the

S.A.V.E.R.S. is presented in unique ways that are results oriented, practical, and have proven to be effective.

One of the most encouraging aspects of the Miracle Morning is that you can implement all six of these powerful personal development practices in one simple, sequential routine that takes as little as six minutes, as much as an hour, or anywhere in between. For your reference, roughly 70 percent of Miracle Morning practitioners schedule 60 minutes to complete their S.A.V.E.R.S., about 20 percent schedule 30 minutes, and the remaining 10 percent spend more or less time on their routine. Whether you choose to allocate 6 minutes to your S.A.V.E.R.S., 60, or somewhere in between, you will have completed all six of these proven personal development practices before the rest of your day even starts.

In the coming pages, we'll dive deeper into each of the S.A.V.E.R.S, and I'll show you how to combine them to gain access to more of your potential, which you can then apply to changing, improving, or completely transforming any aspect of your life.

S Is for Silence

"In the attitude of silence the soul finds the path in a clearer light, and what is elusive and deceptive resolves itself into crystal clearness."
—Mahatma Gandhi

"You can learn more in an hour of silence than you can in a year from books."
—Matthew Kelly

Our lives have become noisier than ever. From the moment we open our eyes until the moment we lay down to bed, most of us are overstimulated, distracted, and overwhelmed.

Silence is the first practice of the S.A.V.E.R.S. and may be one of the most significant areas of improvement to counteract our fast-paced lifestyles. I'm referring to the daily practice of what I call *purposeful* silence. By this, I simply mean that you are engaging in a period of silence with a highly beneficial purpose in mind—not just to pass the time. During periods of purposeful silence, our self-awareness is heightened, and we are primed to experience our most profound insights and ideas.

In the past, these moments of quiet contemplation were built into daily lives. Whether waiting in line, sitting at the airport, going for a walk, or staring out the window on a bus, we had time to listen to our thoughts. Now, due to our smartphones, that kind of solitude, which most people call "boredom," has all but disappeared. Whether we're texting, playing games, checking emails, watching videos, shopping, or mindlessly scrolling through social media, our digital devices have ensured that we never have to be alone with our thoughts. Unfortunately, it would seem that our modern society has lost sight of the profound need for and benefits of having periods of peaceful, purposeful silence built into our lives.

How Do Your Mornings Usually Begin?

When you first wake up, do you invest time in centering yourself and fostering an optimal mental, emotional, and spiritual state to lead you through the rest of the day? Or do you typically wait to wake up until you've got something you need to do, start the day by reaching for your smartphone, and almost immediately begin to flood your mind with external stimuli?

A comprehensive research study conducted by the International Data Corporation (IDC) found that roughly 80 percent of smartphone users check their mobile phones within 15 minutes of waking up, and many within seconds. According to Dr. Nikole Benders-Hadi, a psychiatrist who specializes in neurology, "immediately turning to your phone when you wake up can start your day off in a way that is more likely to increase stress and leave you feeling overwhelmed."

Regardless of how soon you reach for your phone, mornings for most of us are either hectic and stressful, unfocused and unproductive, or a little bit of both. While some of us are rushing to get ready for the day, others are struggling to get going. For many of us, our minds are bombarded with overwhelming internal chatter about what we have to do today, what we didn't get done yesterday, our never-ending to-do list, where we have to go, who we have to see, a recent argument with our spouse, or otherwise worrying about countless things that are out of our immediate control. Thus, we feel out of control, which perpetuates feelings of stress and anxiety.

For others, just getting going in the morning can be an uphill battle. Many start the day feeling sluggish, lazy, and unfocused, and it may take a while to wake up and get going. This isn't the most productive way to start your day and achieve your goals either.

Thankfully, there is a better way. Your Miracle Morning will ensure you have a daily method for quieting your mind, calming your nervous system, reducing your stress, feeling at peace, improving your mental and emotional well-being, and consistently experiencing heightened clarity that will allow you to focus on what's most important in your life.

The benefits of spending time in silence have been well documented throughout the ages. From the power of prayer to the miracle of meditation, some of the greatest minds in history have used purposeful silence to transcend their limitations and create extraordinary results. In his book *Three Simple Steps*, author Trevor Blake refers to this as "taking quiet time":

> In the stories of self-made men and women, I was fascinated that most had some method of escaping the craziness of their schedules to sit quietly somewhere just to contemplate. They claimed their best ideas came to them when they stopped pondering the problem. They all had different ways of describing the process, depending on what was acceptable to believe at the time. The common elements for their systems of idea creation were contemplation time taken alone and, where possible, far from the madding crowd, daily practice, early in the day, and informal.

Here are some of the most common practices to choose from and incorporate into your period of purposeful silence (in no particular order):

- Meditation
- Prayer
- Gratitude
- Breathwork
- Contemplation

Each of these practices will help you to quiet your mind, create space for you to receive wisdom from within (or above), and allow you to be more present and open to experiencing the benefits that will come from the remaining S.A.V.E.R.S.

Some mornings I do just one of the activities listed above, but most mornings I do more than one, often by combining them. For example, I almost always begin my Miracle Morning with a prayer of gratitude and then meditate for anywhere from 5 to 20 minutes, depending on what I feel I need on any given day. My meditation usually begins with some light breathwork by simply focusing on and following my breath as a way to calm my mind. We'll go into that more here in a minute. Note: I also keep my journal next to me so that I can write down any ideas that emerge during my meditation. The mental clarity and ideas that are generated while meditating are sometimes the most valuable aspect of my practice.

I recommend getting out of bed and preferably leaving your bedroom altogether as you begin your S.A.V.E.R.S. Otherwise, it can be too tempting to go from sitting in silence to slouching to falling back asleep. To avoid this temptation, I do my Miracle Morning sitting upright on my living room couch, where I keep everything else I need for my Miracle Morning already set up and waiting for me. My journal, yoga mat, a printout of my affirmations, and the book

I'm currently reading always stay in the same spot so that it's easy to jump right in and engage in my S.A.V.E.R.S. without having to search for anything.

Beginning with Meditation

While meditation is often thought of as a spiritual practice, as of this writing, there are over 1,400 scientific studies that have demonstrated its profound mental, emotional, and physiological benefits. Many of these studies link having a consistent meditation practice to sustained improvements in brain activity, metabolism, blood pressure, and other bodily functions. Meditation can help to lower stress and anxiety, alleviate physical pain, promote better sleep, improve mood, focus, and concentration, and even increase lifespan. In fact, it was an article about Fortune 500 CEOs who attributed their professional and financial success to their meditation practice that convinced me to try it for myself.

There are many forms of meditation and a variety of techniques to choose from, but you can separate all of them into two categories: *guided* and *self-directed*. Guided meditations are those in which you listen to another person's voice and receive instructions to guide your thoughts, attention, and awareness. You can find these online on sites like YouTube, as well as using apps like Calm, Headspace, and the Miracle Morning app. Self-directed meditations are simply those you do on your own without assistance from anyone else.

During the past 15 years, I've explored and experimented with countless types of meditation. This led to me combining various methods to create what I've found to be the most effective form. As you'll notice with my approach to all of the S.A.V.E.R.S., my underlying intention is to make each practice practical, actionable, and results oriented. The following section walks you through a simple step-by-step (self-directed) Emotional Optimization Meditation practice that you can begin implementing immediately, even if you've never meditated before.

Emotional Optimization Meditation

While many meditation techniques center around clearing your mind, observing your thoughts, or following your breath (all of which are effective methods), Emotional Optimization Meditation is the act of consciously choosing which mental and emotional state(s) you wish to experience, and then meditating while in those states to hardwire them into your nervous system. We can all agree that we want to feel *good* (happy, grateful, peaceful, confident, motivated, energized, excited, loved, appreciated, etc.), but most of us allow external circumstances to determine how we feel inside. That, or we allow how we've always felt to continue, even if it doesn't serve us. This meditation enables you to choose how you feel, regardless of your external circumstances or how you've felt up until this point.

You can choose to embody inner peace, freedom, self-love, forgiveness, surrender, self-confidence, or any other state you want to experience more of. Your choice might be based on what you need at any particular moment of your life such as generating feelings of love toward your spouse after an argument, confidence for an upcoming presentation, or even embracing feelings of sadness and grief if that's appropriate for a situation you're dealing with. Or your choice might be an ongoing upgrade to your overall mental and emotional well-being. Generally, the latter—an upgrade to your overall mental and emotional well-being—is what we're after. Whatever you choose, Emotional Optimization Meditation reinforces your desired states so that, eventually, they become your default way of being, feeling, and experiencing life. The more consistently you meditate while in your optimal states (ideally every morning), the more natural it will feel, and the easier it will be to access and remain in those states indefinitely.

Meditation is also an opportunity for you to give yourself permission to let go of your compulsive need to constantly be thinking about something. Much of our thinking is repetitive and unproductive. We either relive the past, worry about the future, or ruminate over our problems—all of which take us out of the present moment. Consider that life *is* the present moment. What we allow ourselves to focus on in each moment becomes our experience of life. So, when we relive the past or worry about the future, we miss out on living fully in the present. Meditation gives you an opportunity to take a break from worrying about your problems and to be fully present to the miracle that is your life.

Lastly, it's important to establish appropriate expectations for your practice. If you are expecting your mind to be completely clear or to have a profound experience each time you sit down to meditate, you will likely be disappointed. It would be similar to expecting to lose 10 pounds every time you did a workout. The reason you meditate is to gradually train yourself to be at peace with your thoughts and emotions, to practice being fully present in each moment, to improve your ability to focus and concentrate, and to optimize your mental and emotional state.

Before you begin your meditation, set up a supportive environment. Find a quiet, comfortable place to sit. You can sit up straight on a couch, on a chair, cross-legged on the floor, or on the edge of a pillow to elevate your spine and provide added comfort. You can close your eyes, or you can choose an object in the room to focus on, whichever you prefer. I recommend deciding on how long you want to meditate and setting a timer that will gently remind you when you've reached your time. If you're brand-new to meditation, I would start with at least 10 minutes, and ideally more, to give your mind time to settle down and so that you don't feel rushed.

Here are three steps to completing an Emotional Optimization Meditation. I recommend reading through all three steps first and then coming back to implement them.

1. **Choose your optimal mental or emotional state.**
    Remember, the objective of this meditation is to consciously choose and then condition your optimal mental and emotional state(s). While it's normal to think that the way we feel is determined by external forces, that is only true if you continue to allow it to be. This meditation is about realizing that you have the power to choose how you experience each moment of your life— regardless of your circumstances—and then exercising that power each day.

    Begin by asking yourself, "Which mental or emotional state would best serve me right now?" How do you want to feel? What's on your agenda for today, and which internal state will enable you to show up at your best for yourself and others?

    Sometimes we need to let go of a negative mental or emotional state before we can embody the optimal states we desire. If you're under a lot of pressure and feeling stressed or overwhelmed, you may find it helpful or even necessary to give yourself permission to let go of those stressful thoughts and feelings in order to be at peace and cultivate your optimal state. If you find this to be the case, ask yourself, "Is there anything I need to let go of?" If there is, be willing to let it go, at least for the duration of your meditation.

    Similarly, if you've been feeling unhappy as of late, you may need to give yourself permission to be happy for the simple reason that you deserve to be happy. No one else can give you that permission; only you can give it to yourself. Even when life is difficult, unpleasant, or painful, we can choose to focus on what we're grateful for and generate genuine feelings of happiness.

Depending on how long it's been since you consistently felt the state you're choosing, it may feel foreign, inauthentic, or difficult at first. For example, if it's been a while since you've felt happy or confident, you may need to think of something that makes you happy or remember the last time you felt confident to be able to bring those feelings into the present. Remember, like with exercising, the results don't come immediately, but gradually. Stick with it, and it will get easier over time.

Don't limit yourself. You deserve to feel however you choose to feel. How do you want to feel today? What is your optimal mental and emotional state? Don't overthink it. Choose any positive state that would be beneficial for you to experience and give yourself permission to experience it. You're going to direct your attention and energy toward generating that state during your meditation.

2. **Focus on your breath to calm your mind.**
    For most people, the biggest obstacle to meditation is the mind's nonstop internal chatter, which is why simple breathing meditations have stood the test of time. The purpose of focusing on your breath is that it draws your attention away from your inner dialogue, enables you to be present to what's happening in the moment, and allows your mind to calm down.

    Begin your meditation by directing your focus toward your breath. Breathe naturally but slowly. Take long, slow inhalations in through the nose followed by long exhalations out through the nose or mouth, whichever feels more comfortable. Although not required, you might also find it helpful to name or count your breaths. An example of naming your breaths would be thinking to yourself, *in ... in ... in ... in ...* during each inhalation, and *out ... out ... out ... out ...* during each exhalation. Counting your breaths is exactly what it sounds like. Some people choose to count each inhalation and exhalation as one breath. I prefer to slowly count *one ... one ... one ... one ...* on the inhale, followed by *two ... two ... two ... two ...* on the exhale, then *three ... three ... three ... three ...* on the next inhale, and so on. Usually, by the time I get to about 20 (which is 10 full inhalations and exhalations), my mind is calmer, and I'm ready to move to the third step.

While you may find that quieting your mind is initially difficult to do (which is normal, to be expected, and serves as evidence that this is an area of growth for you), you'll likely begin to feel your thoughts and emotions gradually settle down as you continue to follow your breath. The key is to not get annoyed or impatient with your unquiet mind. When you catch your attention wandering from your breath to your thoughts, simply acknowledge the shift, be at peace with it, and return to focusing on your breath. Learning to focus your attention and be at peace with your thoughts is a skill. As with any skill, the more you practice, the easier it will become. By the end of your Miracle Morning 30-Day Journey that you'll be receiving in Chapter 10, you'll likely be surprised at how much better you'll be at this.

3. **Meditate in your optimal state.**
    Now that your mind is calmer and hopefully a bit quieter, it's time to direct your attention toward generating the

optimal mental and emotional state that you've chosen. To do this, rather than attempting to empty your mind (like most meditations would have you do), you can actually fill it with thoughts, images, and affirmations that are in alignment with the state you want to experience. For example, let's say your chosen state is "gratitude." As you continue to take slow, calming, deep breaths, you can think to yourself, *I have so much to be grateful for. I am grateful that I am safe in this moment. I am grateful that I have the ability to meditate. I am grateful for the people in my life who love me and whom I get to love. I am grateful for my spiritual connection with God. I am grateful that I have a roof over my head, food to eat, clothes to wear, and so much more. I am grateful for my challenges because they enable me to learn, grow, and become a better version of myself. I am grateful that, no matter what happens to me, I can always choose to be at peace with what I can't change and generate my optimal mental and emotional state,* and so on.

While the above isn't intended to be a script (although you can certainly use it as one), it is an example of how you get to choose what you focus on, and the way you can intentionally bombard your mind with thoughts that direct your consciousness toward generating optimal mental and emotional states.

I also recommend aligning your physiology (breathing, body posture, and facial expression) with your desired state. Continuing with the gratitude example, smile subtly (lips together) as you think of all the things you have to be grateful for. According to a recent study in the journal *Experimental Psychology*, the act of smiling triggers brain chemicals related to positivity, even when the smile isn't genuine at first. If, instead, you've chosen confidence or motivation as your optimal state, sit up straight (or stand), put your shoulders back, and breathe as someone would who is feeling confident and motivated. Embody your optimal state fully.

For the duration of your meditation, continue to direct your thoughts and feelings toward your chosen state. And similar to the breathing portion of the meditation, if your thoughts wander or become contradictory (it's normal to think something positive to yourself and immediately have your subconscious contradict it), simply acknowledge the unsupportive thought(s) and keep replacing them with positive, supportive ones. Again, the more you practice this meditation, the more natural this will become.

Although I still practice other forms of meditation, Emotional Optimization Meditation is my favorite, because it not only calms my mind, it enables me to put myself into a peak mental and emotional state every single day, regardless of what's going on in my life. The longer you practice, the easier it becomes, and the more the benefits compound.

Spending time in silence can be an opportunity for you to be at peace, to experience gratitude, and be free from your day-to-day stressors and worries. And remember, if you'd like to try guided audio meditations so that someone else will lead you through the practice, there are countless varieties available for free on YouTube as well as in the Miracle Morning app.

Personally, I found guided meditations to be helpful when I was starting out because sitting in silence—especially meditating—was quite challenging for me. Listening to other people lead me through what to focus on, what to let go of, and teaching me how to meditate was extremely helpful. It took me three or four weeks of alternating between guided and self-directed meditations before I started to feel like I was getting the hang of it. I finally got to a place where I could allow thoughts to come in; I'd peacefully acknowledge them and then quietly let them drift away without getting frustrated. So, don't be discouraged if spending time in silence or meditating is challenging at first. Stick with it, and the benefits for your life will be invaluable.

A Is for Affirmations

"It's the repetition of affirmations that leads to belief. Once that belief becomes a deep conviction, things begin to happen."
—**Muhammad Ali**

"You will be a failure until you impress the subconscious with the conviction you are a success. This is done by making an affirmation, which clicks."
—**Florence Scovel Shinn**

I am the greatest!" Muhammad Ali affirmed these words over and over again—and then he *became* them. What we repeatedly tell or affirm to ourselves becomes our internal reality and impacts our ability to affect our external reality. Thus, affirmations are one of the most effective tools to articulate the person you need to be to achieve everything you want in your life, and then become that person.

Every one of us has an internal dialogue that runs almost non-stop through our minds. The problem is that most of what we think is unconscious, meaning we don't actively and intentionally choose our internal dialogue. As a result, we allow our past experiences and limitations to replay in our heads. Doing this reaffirms and perpetuates our limiting beliefs in ourselves and the world around us. Although this is a "normal" thing that we all do, it can be one of the most detrimental factors holding us back from fulfilling our potential. As Henry Ford famously said, "Whether you think you can, or you think you can't, you're right."

How's Your Mental Programming?

We've all been programmed—at the subconscious level—to think, believe, and behave the way we do. Our programming is a result of many influences, including what we have been told by others, what we have told ourselves, and all our life experiences—both good and bad. Some of us have programming that makes it relatively easy for us to be happy and successful, while others—possibly the majority—have programming that can make life more difficult than it needs to be.

The *bad news* is that if you don't consciously design and choose your inner dialogue, you can easily fall victim to repeating and reliving the fears, insecurities, and limitations of your past. When we constantly focus on what we're doing wrong and where we're falling short, we can cause ourselves to feel guilty, inadequate, and undeserving of the success we really want.

The *good news* is that our programming can be changed or improved at any time. We can immediately begin to reprogram our minds to overcome all our fears, insecurities, and past limitations so that we can become as successful as we choose to be, in any area of our lives. I'm going to walk you through a simple but powerful step-by-step formula to create written affirmations designed to produce meaningful results (not just make you feel better). You'll be able to identify, articulate, and affirm what you're committed to accomplishing and experiencing in your life, why it's a must for you, and which specific actions you're going to take to accomplish it. With enough repetition, your subconscious mind will begin to believe what you tell it, act upon it, and eventually, create your intentionally chosen reality.

It is imperative that you draft your affirmations in writing—either on paper or digitally. This way, you can carefully craft them using precise language so that they are authentic and tailored to you. Everyone's desired outcomes are different, as are the self-imposed limitations that are getting in the way, so it only makes sense that the language you choose should resonate with you. Another benefit of writing them down is that you can recite them every day. It's through this repetition that your mind begins to accept the possibility of a new reality for you. It's the constant repetition of an affirmation that spurs the action necessary to make real change in your life.

Why the Old Way of Doing Affirmations Doesn't Work

We can clearly see that affirmations, when done correctly, have proven to be highly effective at transforming our thoughts and behaviors. But affirmations have also gotten a bad rap. They're often viewed as ineffective, at best, or totally cheesy, at worst. For decades, countless well-meaning self-help experts and gurus have taught affirmations in ways that are ineffective and unintentionally set people up for failure. Many people have tried them only to be disappointed.

When I was younger, I was among the crowd who considered affirmations to be both cheesy *and* ineffective. I thought they were a lot of feel-good statements that had zero grounding in reality and that just deluded people into feeling better in the moment. Those of us who are results oriented and, you know, sane, didn't bother repeating feel-good statements just to mask our insecurities. I had no confidence that they would produce results.

My first real-life exposure to the power of affirmations came when I was living with one of my closest and most successful friends, Matt Recore. Nearly every day, I would hear Matt shouting from the shower in his bedroom. Thinking he was yelling for me, I would approach his bedroom door only to find that he was shouting things like, "I am in control of my destiny! I deserve to be a success! I am committed to doing everything I must do today to reach my goals and create the life of my dreams!" *What a weirdo*, I thought.

The only previous exposure I had to affirmations was through a popular 1990s spoof on the hit TV show *Saturday Night Live* in which Al Franken's character Stuart Smalley hosted a fictitious show called *Daily Affirmations with Stuart Smalley*. He began each episode by staring into a mirror and repeating to himself, "I'm good enough, I'm smart enough, and doggone it, people like me!" The bit was funny, but it also made me believe that affirmations weren't to be taken seriously.

Fortunately for Matt, he knew better. As a longtime student of Tony Robbins, Matt had been using affirmations and incantations for years to carefully program his subconscious mind and create extraordinary levels of success. As a self-made millionaire who owned five homes (all by age 25), Matt clearly knew what he was doing. Had I been paying closer attention, I might have made the connection between Matt's yelling in the shower and his success. After all, I was the one renting a room in *his* house. Unfortunately, it took me a few more years to realize that affirmations were one of the most powerful tools for personal transformation.

As I began studying personal development, I was reintroduced to affirmations as a legitimate tool for transformation. The promise was that affirmations could change my life by repeating them until I believed them. For someone who grew up believing I was lazy (because I was), that sounded right up my alley. *I don't have to do anything*, I thought. I was all in.

Until I wasn't. It didn't take long for me to hit the same brick wall with my affirmations that most people come up against.

Nothing happened when I used the format that was commonly taught by pioneers in the self-help field. That great life I kept talking about didn't appear. Using "I am" statements to affirm I was something that I wasn't felt inauthentic.

Then, one day, I had an epiphany. I realized that the flaw wasn't in affirmations themselves. They had simply been misunderstood, mistaught, and misused. I eventually narrowed the flaws down to two that were significant, which enabled me to completely change my approach and design affirmations that were practical, actionable, and consistently produced tangible, measurable results.

In the following pages, I'll give you a step-by-step formula to create your own Miracle Morning results-oriented affirmations that are rooted in truth and strategically designed to reprogram your subconscious mind and help direct your conscious behavior. Before we get to that, let's take a minute to explore these two flaws and the problems that they cause.

Flaw 1: Lying to Yourself Doesn't Work

"I am a millionaire." Are you? "I have 7 percent body fat." Do you? "I have achieved all of my goals this year." Have you?

Wording your affirmations as if you've already achieved, overcome, or become something that you haven't (yet) may be the single biggest reason that affirmations are ineffective for most people. This technique teaches us to repeatedly affirm something that we *wish* were true in the hope that we trick ourselves into believing it. Deep down, if these statements aren't true, then you *know* they're not true. And every time you recite an affirmation that isn't rooted in truth, you are lying to yourself, and your subconscious mind will resist or reject it. If you affirm "I am wealthy" or "I am happy" when that doesn't resonate as true for you, you're going to create an unnecessary inner conflict (as if we need one more).

Given that you're an intelligent human being who isn't delusional, lying to yourself repeatedly will never be the optimal strategy. The truth will always prevail.

Flaw 2: Passive Language Doesn't Produce Meaningful Results

Many affirmations have been designed to make us feel good in the moment by creating an empty promise of something we desire, independent of any effort. For example, here is a popular money-related affirmation that's been perpetuated by many well-meaning spiritual teachers and self-help authorities: "I am a money magnet. Money flows to me effortlessly and in abundance."

If only making money were that simple. Sign me up!

If we're going to take time to recite affirmations, we'd like to see them produce meaningful results, not merely delude us into momentarily feeling better. If we're reciting an affirmation about improving our financial situation, we want to see our income or bank account balance begin to increase. If we're repeating an affirmation about losing weight, we want the results of that affirmation to show up every time we step on the scale. If we're using affirmations to improve our marriage, we want our spouse to experience (and ideally, reciprocate) the improvements we've made.

In order to achieve concrete results, our affirmations must lead to changes in our behaviors. That's why passive language affirmations are ineffective.

3 Steps to Creating Miracle Morning Results-Oriented Affirmations

Creating affirmations that enable you to improve any area of your life isn't complicated—it's a matter of understanding the approach that'll get you there. There are three simple steps you can follow to create practical, actionable, results-oriented affirmations that effectively reprogram your subconscious mind and redirect your conscious thoughts to align your behavior so you can achieve your goals and make the changes you want to make in your life.

Step 1: Affirm What You're Committed To

Notice we're not starting with what you *want*. We all want countless things, but we only get what we're committed to. One could even argue that the single most determining factor in whether we reach any goal or make any meaningful change in our lives is our ability to fully commit to something, and to remain committed for as long as it takes. When you're committed, there is always a way. However, most people struggle to make new commitments beyond what they're already doing. Thus, nothing changes.

Repeatedly affirming what you're committed to, every single day, both keeps your commitment top of mind and consistently increases your level of commitment over time. So, each of your affirmations should first clearly articulate exactly which *outcome* (goal, result, improvement, etc.) or *activity* (action, habit, ritual, etc.) you are committed to experiencing in your life. To help clarify the difference between an outcome and an activity: an outcome would be "losing 10 pounds." An activity would be "exercising five days a week."

Here's what that looks like in the form of a written affirmation:

> I am committed to _____ no
> matter what—there is no other option!

The more consistently you affirm what you're committed to, with conviction, the more committed you will become to making it happen.

You may notice that there is an exclamation point (!) after the affirmation. That is intentional, as it reminds me to read and embody it with emotion and conviction. Real commitment isn't something you do haphazardly. The more you can embody your affirmations with emotion and conviction, the more effective they will be.

Your Turn: Apply Step 1 to Your Affirmations

What do you want to accomplish or change in your life that you need to commit to? Do you have an important goal that you've been putting off? Is there an area of your life that is a source of pain and frustration? Is there a change you've attempted to make but haven't succeeded (yet)?

Start by writing down a specific, meaningful outcome or activity—one that challenges you, would significantly improve your life, and that you are ready to commit to—even if you're not exactly sure how you will do it or you're feeling afraid of falling short.

You can handwrite your affirmation in a journal or on a piece of paper, but I recommend using a digital device, such as a notes app on your computer, phone, or the free Miracle Morning Routine app (which has a built-in affirmations creator that follows these three steps). What I like best about using a digital device is that it enables you to go back and easily update your affirmations as often as you'd like, since, as you continue to learn, grow, and evolve, your affirmations should evolve as well.

Once you've identified a meaningful outcome or activity you need to commit to in order to make it a reality, then write or type it using the following (step 1) template to fill in the blank and make it your own:

I am committed to _____ no
matter what—there is no other option!

Whatever goes in that blank is up to you. If you're feeling unsure or hesitant about what you want, you may be censoring yourself because of a lack of clarity or a lack of confidence in your ability to commit and follow through. That's totally normal. However, you don't have to have everything figured out to begin your affirmation. In fact, it is often after you commit to something that the *how* reveals itself. You figure it out along the way. Writing down your affirmation is the first step in establishing your commitment, then affirming your commitment each day keeps it top of mind and consistently increases your level of commitment over time. Remember: *there's always a way when you're committed.*

Step 2: Affirm Why It's Important to You

Next, it is time to support, enhance, and reinforce your commitment by including your *why*—the deeply meaningful, compelling reason(s) that will continuously fuel you to stay committed and take the necessary actions until what you're affirming becomes your reality. Why is this commitment meaningful to you? Why is it a must for you? In what ways will it enhance your life and/or the lives of those you care about? The more compelling the reason(s) you have to follow through with your commitment, the more likely you are to follow through.

Your Turn: Apply Step 2 to Your Affirmations

Let's continue drafting your affirmation. Underneath your commitment (step 1), begin listing the reasons that following through with this commitment is important to you. Again, why is it meaningful to you? Why is it a must for you? In what ways will it enhance your life and/or the lives of those you care about? What are the most compelling reasons/benefits that will keep you inspired to do whatever it takes?

I am committed to _____ for/because:

- _____ [Insert meaningful reason/benefit]
- _____ [Insert meaningful reason/benefit]
- _____ [Insert meaningful reason/benefit]

Keep in mind that these reasons are personal to you, and you'll never have to share your affirmations with anyone else, unless of course you want to. Also, remember that this is your rough draft. You can always edit your affirmations, so don't worry about getting anything perfect. A poorly written affirmation is far more effective than a nonexistent affirmation.

Step 3: Affirm Which Actions You'll Take and When

Writing an affirmation that merely states the outcome you're committed to and why it's important to you, without clarifying the necessary actions that will produce the outcome, is one notch above pointless. It can also be counterproductive, tricking your subconscious mind into thinking that the result will happen automatically, without any effort.

In this third and final step, you'll simply ask yourself what you need to do to achieve your ideal outcome, clarify the specific action(s) that are required for you to follow through with your commitment, and clearly state when and how often you will execute the necessary action. This step may be obvious and come to you quickly. Very often, we already know what we need to do to improve, we just haven't committed to doing it.

My sixth and final year working for Cutco, I set a monumental goal of doubling my best year ever in sales. While attempting to double my sales (and income) was extremely intimidating, I realized that to achieve it, I simply needed to double the number of phone calls I made to prospects. Twice as many calls should mean twice as many appointments scheduled, which should theoretically result in twice as many sales. Having averaged roughly 10 calls per day during my previous best year in sales, I determined that if I increased my calls to 20 per day, then I would inevitably double my sales. I knew what I needed to do; I had just never committed to doing it (at that level) before. So, I made a commitment to simply schedule time to make 20 calls each day from 8 to 9 AM, no matter what. At the end of the year, I had followed through with my commitment and more than doubled my sales, which more than doubled my income from the previous year.

However, depending on your desired outcome, you may have little to no idea what you need to do to get started. In that case, the initial action you'll commit to taking will be scheduling time to figure out which other actions you need to take. For example, let's say you've always wanted to start your own business or you desperately want to save your marriage, but you're not sure how to do it. In that case, your first action is scheduling time to figure out the next steps. A simple Google search for "How to start a business" or "How to save my marriage" can get you started. Of course, there is an endless supply of resources (articles, YouTube videos, podcasts, etc.) available for free on just about any topic, and to go deeper, there are countless books available from authors and experts who have experience with whatever you're trying to accomplish.

Here are a few examples of different goals you might have and specific actions you could take to meet them:

To ensure that I follow through with my commitment to increase my income and provide financial security for my family, I will schedule time to implement the following actions:

- Read books on how to make more money, every single day, so that I can learn effective strategies to model.
- Find a local business networking group and join it.
- Make 20 prospecting calls per day, five days per week, from 8 to 9 AM.

To ensure that I follow through with my commitment to optimize my health, I will schedule time to implement the following actions:

- Practice intermittent fasting and start each day with a low-sugar, organic, plant-based smoothie that's high in healthy fats.
- Exercise for 10 minutes every morning, during my Miracle Morning. And when the weather is nice, go for a 10-minute walk every day after dinner.
- Finish my last meal three to four hours before bed so that my body can fully digest my food before sleeping.

To ensure that I follow through with my commitment to be the best husband I can be for my spouse, I will schedule time to implement the following actions:

- Read books on marriage every morning, before reading any other books, so that I can continuously learn how to be the best spouse I can possibly be.
- Every morning, I will identify at least one thing I can do that day to either enhance my wife's life or

make it easier in some way (e.g., get her flowers or a card, give her a massage, write her a love note, go on a walk together, do the dishes, pick up the kids from school, play a board game, sit and talk in the evening, watch our favorite show together, etc.).

· I will bring romance and connection back into our relationship by scheduling a date night twice a month on Wednesday nights (to avoid the weekend rush).

Your Turn: Apply Step 3 to Your Affirmations

As you implement this third and final step, keep the following in mind:

- Some actions may be repetitive and recurring (like when I committed to making 20 calls per day, five days per week, from 8 to 9 AM to double my sales), while others may be sequential (step 1, step 2, step 3, etc.).
- If you're not sure which actions you need to take, simply affirm when you will schedule time to discover and determine what those actions will be. You don't need to have everything figured out to get started. In fact, that false belief is often what prevents us from getting started in the first place.
- Keep this as simple as possible. Don't overwhelm yourself.

The more specific your actions are, the better. Be sure to include frequency (how often) and precise time frames to clarify when you will begin and end your actions.

To ensure that I follow through with my commitment,
I will implement the following actions at these specified
times/frequencies:

- _____
- _____
- _____

Putting It All Together (Step 1 + Step 2 + Step 3)

The key to achieving any goal or improving any aspect of your life is harnessing your ability to make a commitment and maintain that commitment for as long as it takes, even when you don't feel like it. Your Miracle Morning results-oriented affirmations are designed to help you do exactly that by ensuring that you stay focused on what you're committed to improving or achieving in your life, why each improvement or achievement is so important to you that you're willing to do whatever is necessary to do it, and which specific actions you'll take (and when) to ensure that you follow through.

As I said earlier, my experience has been that affirmations, when approached in the ways outlined in this chapter, are the most effective form of personal development. They allow you total precision when designing your present and future reality. So, choose one area of your life that you want to improve, or your most important goal, and follow these three steps to write an affirmation that will keep you focused on what matters most to you.

Tips to Maximize the Effectiveness of Your Affirmations

- **Consider creating additional affirmations beyond this formula.** In its simplest form, an affirmation is merely a _reminder_ of something you deem important that you want to embody or integrate into your life. This results-oriented affirmation formula reminds you of *what you're committed to, why it's a must for you, and which specific actions you'll take (and when).* However, other styles of affirmations can also be useful, so long as they're rooted in truth. "I choose to be happy" is an affirmation. "I am at peace with what I can't change" is an affirmation. "I am exactly where I am supposed to be to learn what I need to learn to become the person I need to be to create the life I want" is an affirmation. In fact, one of my favorite affirmations doesn't follow this formula at all. It reads, "I am just as worthy, deserving, and capable of creating the life I'm committed to as any other person on earth, and I will prove that today with my actions." This foundational affirmation helps me to overcome my insecurities and imposter syndrome by reminding me that *all* of us are inherently just as worthy, deserving, and capable of whatever we are willing to fully commit to. So, while I recommend using the three-step formula taught in this chapter to create results-oriented affirmations that will help you achieve your goals and make significant improvements, don't feel that you are constrained by it. Feel free to affirm whatever you deem important, and that you want to keep top of mind.

- **Update your affirmations as needed.** Keep in mind that your affirmations will likely never be a final draft because as you continue to learn, grow, and evolve, your affirmations should evolve as well. When you come up with a new goal, dream, habit, or philosophy you want to integrate into your life, create an affirmation to support it. When you accomplish a goal or completely integrate a new habit or philosophy into your life, you might find that it's no longer necessary to affirm it every day, and thus you can choose to remove it from your written affirmations.

Regularly updating your affirmations also keeps them from getting stale and you from getting bored. This is why I recommend typing your affirmations on a digital device, such as your computer or phone. That way you can update them as often as you'd like.

- **Read your affirmations daily.** It's important to be consistent with reading your affirmations, *ideally at least once a day*. Reading an affirmation occasionally is as effective as getting an occasional workout. You're unlikely to see any measurable results until you make it a part of your daily routine. The more often you read them, the faster they will reprogram your subconscious and upgrade your habitual thought patterns so that your thinking will be in alignment with how you want to feel (good) and what you want to do (be productive).

- **Recite your affirmations with emotion.** When you recite your affirmations, whether out loud or in your head, I recommend putting yourself in a heightened emotional state to reinforce your conviction and commitment. Remember, your Miracle Morning affirmations aren't intended to be read just for the sake of reading them. These are thoughtfully crafted statements, strategically engineered to program your subconscious mind and upgrade your identity with the beliefs, perspectives, and commitment you need to achieve your desired outcomes, while directing your conscious mind to keep you focused on your highest priorities and the actions that will get you there. For your affirmations to be optimally effective, it is important that you engage your emotions while reciting them. Mindlessly repeating an affirmation without intentionally feeling your commitment to it will have minimal impact. You must take responsibility for generating authentic emotions, such as excitement and determination, and powerfully infusing those emotions with every affirmation you recite. If this doesn't come naturally to you, or if you find yourself in a perpetually negative mental and emotional state, such as feeling discouraged or depressed, this may seem easier said than done. This pairs nicely with Emotional Optimization Meditation, as you can use EOM to get yourself in a peak state before reciting your affirmations. Focus on the mental and emotional state(s) you want to experience, and ask yourself, "When was the last time I felt that way? What did it feel like? How would I show up now if I felt that way? What would I think? What would I say to myself? What would I do? How would I move my body?" Then, think, speak, and move as if you were experiencing those heightened emotions. Do this each day during your Miracle Morning, and in time, you will condition yourself to experience those emotions naturally and authentically.

V Is for Visualization

"Ordinary people believe only in the possible. Extraordinary people visualize not what is possible or probable, but rather what is impossible. And by visualizing the impossible, they begin to see it as possible."
—Chérie Carter-Scott

"See things as you would have them be instead of as they are."
—Robert Collier

On May 6, 1954, Roger Bannister became the first human in recorded history to run a mile in under four minutes, finishing in precisely 3:59.4. Before Bannister's unprecedented accomplishment, no one had ever run a sub-four-minute mile, and it was widely believed to be beyond a human's physiological capabilities.

When asked how he accomplished this seemingly impossible feat, he described that, as part of his training, he had relentlessly visualized the achievement to create a sense of certainty in his mind and body. Roger is just one extraordinary example of how we can all use visualization to perform at our best.

Visualization, also known as mental rehearsal, is the process of imagining exactly what you want to achieve or experience, then mentally rehearsing precisely what you need to do to achieve or experience it while generating an optimal emotional state that compels you to do whatever you need to do. It is frequently used by elite athletes and performers to mentally rehearse their work, helping them to prepare and ultimately to perform at peak levels.

Without realizing it, we engage in mental rehearsal almost every day, though often in a way that is detrimental to our success. Every time we think of an unpleasant or difficult task that we don't particularly want to do, we are rehearsing the feelings of *not* wanting to do it. If you think to yourself, "I'm supposed to go to the gym today after work, but I really don't want to go," then when five o'clock rolls around, the mindset and resulting emotions you unconsciously rehearsed earlier in the day are likely to determine your behavior in the moment. This is how we consistently rehearse *not* doing what we need to do, and then we often end up not doing it. Thinking ourselves out of doing what we need to do becomes an unconscious habit that robs us of everything we want to create for our lives.

Visualization is our antidote to this unconscious and destructive habit, which can be implemented in just a few minutes each morning. However, much like affirmations, it can be counterproductive when done ineffectively.

The Problems with Visualization and Vision Boards
Ever since the bestselling book and documentary *The Secret* made its way into pop culture in 2006, a method of visualization has been popularized that can be both ineffective and counterproductive. This method involves visualizing what you want for your life without visualizing yourself engaged in the necessary activities that

will get you there. We are taught to cut out and post pictures of the house, the car, the body, and the life of our dreams. We are told that if we do this, we will "attract" everything we want in our lives.

While vision boarding may be a fun weekend craft project to do with your family, and keeping images of things you aspire to be or have or do is certainly not without value, it is hardly the most effective form of visualization. It also gives people a false sense of hope, encouraging them to believe that their ideal outcome is going to magically become a reality just because they put a bunch of pictures on a poster board. No offense, but this is borderline delusional.

The Benefits of Visualization (for the Rest of Us)

Although elite athletes and performers are typically known to use visualization to perform at their best, I've discovered another benefit that is even more helpful for those of us who aren't competing in the Olympics or performing on Broadway. Visualization can help us overcome one of the biggest obstacles standing between us and accomplishing what we want in our lives: getting ourselves to do what we know we need to do when we don't feel like doing it.

Whether it's due to a lack of inspiration, motivation, or physical energy, we often don't feel like doing what we need to do when we need to do it. We allow our feelings to determine our behavior, which causes us to procrastinate since it's always easier to do nothing or continue doing what we've always done. When you discover how to overcome that obstacle and consistently generate the clarity and motivation you need to take the necessary actions you know you should be taking—when you should be taking them—there is very little that can stop you from realizing your full potential and achieving your goals.

Allow me to share a personal story that illustrates precisely how you'll be able to use visualization to generate the clarity and motivation you need to do what you need to do when you need to do it, whether you feel like it or not.

For most of my life, I hated running. I realize that *hate* is a strong word, and I rarely use it, but I've despised and avoided running for as long as I can remember. I vividly recall dreading having to run the mile in high school PE class. However, in early 2009, after roughly six months of doing the Miracle Morning, I asked myself what a level 10 would be in the category of physical fitness. I decided it would be to run a marathon (26.2 miles). However, I had two friends who had both run ultramarathons (52 miles), and I considered the possibility that if they could do it, *maybe* I could too. Having never run more than a mile (which was against my will in high school P.E. class), I figured that for me to run 52 consecutive miles, I would have to evolve far beyond who I had ever been, both mentally and physically.

Although the prospect of becoming someone who could run an ultramarathon was somewhat exciting, it was also (mostly) terrifying. It just so happened that a charity I sat on the board of, Front Row Foundation, was hosting its annual fundraising run at the Atlantic City Marathon that October. That gave me six months to train. So, I made a commitment to the foundation and announced publicly that I would train for and complete the ultramarathon to raise money for Front Row Foundation. I immediately began using visualization to help me overcome my resistance to running.

First, I spent roughly 60 seconds visualizing my ideal outcome—crossing the finish line of the Atlantic City Marathon—and imagining what it would feel like. The benefits of this were twofold. One, it helped to generate clarity of outcome and made this seemingly impossible accomplishment feel more and more real every time I visualized it. And two, it helped me to fuel my desire and generate motivation to want to make that vision a reality.

Second (and this is key), I visualized exactly what I needed to do *that day* to make progress toward my ideal outcome and did so while putting myself in a peak emotional state that would compel me to take the necessary action. I closed my eyes and vividly pictured my iPhone, resting on our living room coffee table, displaying 7 AM and the alarm beeping to let me know it was time to go for my run. I saw myself stand up off the couch, walk into my bedroom, and head into my closet to get dressed. I pictured myself putting on my running clothes, then heading back out to my living room and toward the front door. I saw myself opening the door, looking at the sidewalk, and smiling as I said to myself with conviction and enthusiasm, "I'm excited to go for a run today because it is enabling me to become the best version of myself!" I repeated these sentiments and created congruent physiology as I nodded my head and generated feelings of excitement to go for today's run.

I didn't wish or want or hope for the feelings I needed to compel me to go for a run; I *generated* those feelings. Within a few short minutes, I had rehearsed myself taking the necessary actions I knew I needed to take to reach my goal, while putting myself in an optimal emotional state that would compel me to take those actions at the predetermined time.

The payoff for this method of visualization was that when the alarm on my phone sounded and the display read 7 AM, I didn't turn it off and think to myself, "Ugh, I hate running. I can just skip today and do it tomorrow." That didn't happen because that's not what I rehearsed. Instead, when my alarm went off, I did exactly what I had visualized that morning, almost automatically and with virtually no resistance. I stood up, went into my closet, got dressed, walked across my living room to the front door, opened the door, and as soon as I saw the sidewalk, I was flooded with the positive emotions that I had generated that morning. Even the same words ran through my head: *I'm excited to go for a run today because it is enabling me to become the best version of myself!* And off I went, suddenly able and compelled to do the thing that I had despised and avoided for my entire life. That's the power and primary benefit of visualization.

3 Steps for Your Miracle Morning Visualization

Although you can do the S.A.V.E.R.S. in any order, there is a nice rhythm to placing visualization directly after your affirmations because you can visualize what you affirmed. After reciting your affirmations is the prime time to visualize yourself acting in alignment with your affirmations. Here are three simple, sequential steps to do that.

Step 1: Prepare Your Mindset

Our mindset sets the tone going into any experience. So, remember that the primary objectives and benefits of your visualization include the following:

- See and feel what it will be like to achieve your ideal outcome so you're able to generate the clarity and motivation that will help fuel your drive to do what's necessary to achieve it.
- Mentally rehearse yourself taking the necessary actions that you've determined you'll need to take to achieve your ideal outcome.
- Do all the above while getting yourself into a peak emotional state so that you'll be far more compelled to follow through with the necessary actions at whatever time you've determined you'll need to take them.

The act of visualizing isn't particularly difficult. Still, some people either overcomplicate it or struggle with it due to their own fears, insecurities, or other mental or emotional obstacles that make visualizing their success uncomfortable. Others may worry what other people will think of them for pursuing their goals or possibly feel guilty that their loved ones will feel left behind.

This famous quote from Marianne Williamson's book *A Return to Love* should resonate with anyone who feels mental or emotional obstacles when attempting to visualize:

> Our deepest fear is not that we are inadequate. Our deepest fear is that we are powerful beyond measure. It is our light, not our darkness that most frightens us. We ask ourselves, 'Who am I to be brilliant, gorgeous, talented, fabulous?' Actually, who are you not to be? You are a child of God. Your playing small does not serve the world. There is nothing enlightened about shrinking so that other people won't feel insecure around you. We are all meant to shine, as children do. We were born to make manifest the glory of God that is within us. It's not just in some of us; it's in everyone. And as we let our own light shine, we unconsciously give other people permission to do the same. As we are liberated from our own fear, our presence automatically liberates others.

Consider that the greatest gift you can give to the people that you love, as well as those that you lead, is to consistently strive to fulfill your potential so that you gain the ability to help them do the same.

It's time to suspend any fears, insecurities, or concerns with what other people think and get into a mindset of possibility. What do *you* really want? Forget about any self-imposed limitations you may have clung to. Remember, you can't go back and change the past, but you can change everything else, starting now. You are just as worthy, deserving, and capable of creating everything you want for your life as any other person on earth. You deserve to be happy, healthy, and financially secure. Now let's visualize what that looks like for you.

Sit up tall, in a comfortable position. This can be on a chair, couch, floor, or the like. Breathe deeply. Close your eyes, clear your mind, and get ready to visualize.

Step 2: Visualize Your Ideal Outcome

When we visualize ourselves experiencing what we want, we stir up emotions that lift our spirits and pull us toward our vision. The more vividly you see what you want, and the more intensely you allow yourself to experience *now* the feelings you will feel once you've achieved your goal, the more you make the possibility of achieving it feel real.

So, let's begin with the end in mind. What's a goal you'd like to achieve? What is an improvement or accomplishment that you would love to see come to fruition?

Your ideal outcome can be a lifelong dream such as writing a book, starting a business, or traveling the world. It can be a short- or long-term goal, such as losing 10 pounds, transforming your marriage, increasing your income, or being happy and enjoying this one life you've been blessed to live. Or it can be as simple and immediate as how you want to greet your spouse or your kids for the day. Whatever your desired outcome, visualization will help you rehearse making it happen so that you're primed to actually make it happen.

Having considered what an ideal outcome would be for you in any area of your life, you're going to simply close your eyes and imagine what it will look and feel like to achieve it. Vividly imagine the positive feelings that moment will bring. For me, it was crossing the finish line of the Atlantic City Marathon. For you, it might be improving your health, growing your business, or connecting more deeply with someone you love.

As you visualize your ideal outcome, make it as vivid as possible. See, feel, hear, touch, taste, and smell every detail of your vision. Involve more than one of your senses to maximize the effectiveness of your visualization. The point is to see yourself accomplishing what you set out to accomplish and to *experience* how good it will feel to have followed through and made your vision a reality. The more vivid you make your vision, the more real it will feel and the more compelled you'll be to take the necessary actions to make it a reality.

Step 3: Visualize Taking the Necessary Actions (While in an Optimal Emotional State)

Once you've spent a few minutes visualizing a clear mental picture of your ideal outcome, showing yourself what's possible and imagining what it will feel like to experience it, the next step is to determine which actions to take to achieve that outcome and then rehearse yourself taking those actions. This step is where you're going to use visualization to overcome what is arguably the most significant obstacle standing between us and creating the lives we want: *getting yourself to do what you need to do, when you need to do it, whether you feel like it or not.* Overcoming that obstacle makes you virtually unstoppable.

We often avoid following through with our most important actions because they either are outside of our comfort zone, carry with them significant consequences that cause some level of fear within us, or are simply easier not to do than to do. This method of visualization is a mental rehearsal that prepares you to take action. It is the practice of seeing yourself engaged in your most consequential actions for *today* while putting yourself into an optimal emotional state that will compel you to take those actions in real time.

Simply close your eyes and see yourself engaged in the activities you've decided you need to do today (exercising, working, researching, writing, making phone calls, engaging with other people in a positive way, etc.), and make sure you envision yourself enjoying the process. See yourself smiling as you're running on that treadmill, filled with a sense of pride for your self-discipline in following through. Picture the look of determination on your face as you make those phone calls, work on that report, or finally take action and make progress on that project you've been putting off for far too long. Generate feelings of love and playfulness as you rehearse greeting your family for the day. Visualize yourself in a peak mental and emotional state, doing whatever you need to do *today* to move in the direction of your ideal outcomes.

E Is for Exercise

"If you don't make time for exercise, you'll probably have to make time for illness."
—Robin Sharma

"The only exercise most people get is jumping to conclusions, running down their friends, side-stepping responsibility, and pushing their luck."
—Unknown

We all know how important exercise is for maintaining our health, increasing our strength, and improving our endurance, but we may not be aware of the benefits that are specific to exercising in the *morning*. The benefits of morning exercise are too significant to ignore. From quickly transcending that just-woke-up mental fog and boosting your alertness, to enhancing your mental clarity and focus, to helping you sustain higher levels of energy throughout the day, exercising soon after rising optimizes how you feel and how well you perform your daily tasks.

When you exercise, even for just a few minutes, it circulates blood and oxygen throughout your body, significantly boosting your energy and cognitive functions, enabling you to think more effectively and concentrate longer. Postponing exercise delays the benefits that would otherwise positively impact your productivity throughout the day.

Additionally, exercising on an empty stomach (in a fasted state) has been proven to burn more excess body fat than exercising after eating a meal. This happens because after a full night's sleep, your supply of carbohydrates (your body's preferred energy source) is not readily available. According to a study performed at the University of Cambridge, "Aerobic exercise at low-to-moderate intensity, performed in the fasted state, induces an increase in fat oxidation when compared with exercise performed following consumption of a carbohydrate-containing meal."

To clarify, I'm not suggesting that you need to go to the gym or do a full-blown workout in the morning. What I am suggesting is that you spend a few minutes moving your body and elevating your heart rate so that you can harness the benefits of morning exercise.

I recently watched an encouraging interview with personal development expert, bestselling author, and entrepreneur Eben Pagan. He was being interviewed by Tony Robbins, who asked, "Eben, what is your number one key to success?" I was pleasantly surprised when Eben's response was, "I start every morning off with a personal success ritual. That is the most important key to success." He then went on to address the importance of morning exercise.

"Every morning, you've got to get your heart rate up and get your blood flowing and fill your lungs with oxygen," he said. "Don't just exercise at the end of the day or in the middle of the day. And even if you do like to exercise at those times, always incorporate at least 10 to 20 minutes of jumping jacks or some sort of aerobic exercise in the morning."

As you customize your Miracle Morning, you'll decide the amount of time you want to devote to exercise, but as you'll see in the next chapter, you can experience the benefits of morning exercise in as little as 60 seconds (literally). For now, just know that whatever you do during your period of morning exercise—whether you spend a few minutes doing jumping jacks, lifting weights, following a yoga video on YouTube, or going for a quick walk, run, or bike ride outside—is up to you. What's important is that you commit to engaging your body in movement during your Miracle Morning to get blood and oxygen circulating throughout your body and brain, so you can think and feel at your best.

Let's Talk About Yoga

To be clear, I am no yogi. But if I were only allowed to practice *one* form of exercise for the rest of my life, I would, without a doubt, choose yoga. The reason is that it is a complete, holistic form of exercise. It is complete in that it combines stretching, strength training, cardiovascular training, breathwork, and even meditation. It is holistic in that it tends to benefit the mind, body, and spirit—simultaneously.

I began practicing yoga shortly after I established my Miracle Morning and have been doing it, and loving it, ever since. One of my favorite teachers has been world-renowned yoga expert and author Dashama. I have found her to be one of the most authentic, enjoyable, and practical yoga teachers I've ever come across. I asked her to share her unique perspective as a true expert who has invested well beyond 10,000 hours into practicing and teaching yoga.

> Yoga is a multifaceted science that has applications for the physical, mental, emotional, and spiritual aspects of life. When Hal asked me to contribute a short introduction to yoga for this book, I felt it was in perfect alignment with *The Miracle Morning*. I know from personal experience that yoga can help you create miracles in your life. I've

experienced it in mine and witnessed it in countless others whom I have taught around the world.

The important thing to remember is that yoga can take place in many forms. Whether it is sitting in silent meditation, breathing to expand your lung capacity, or back bending to open your heart— there are practices that can help every aspect of your life. The key is to learn which techniques to practice when you need a remedy and to use it to your advantage to bring yourself into balance.

A consistent yoga practice can enhance your life in many ways. It can heal what is out of harmony and can move stuck or blocked energy through your body, creating space for new fluid movement, blood flow, and energy to circulate. I encourage you to try some new sequences as you feel ready.

Blessings and love,

Dashama

If you'd like to try yoga from the comfort of your own home, I recommend simply visiting YouTube and searching "yoga" to access countless guided videos from Dashama and other yoga teachers.

Final Thoughts on Exercise

While we all know how beneficial daily exercise is for optimizing our health and energy levels, it can be far too easy to procrastinate and make excuses to put off exercising. Two of the most common excuses are "I don't have time" and "I'm too tired." Have either of those excuses ever stopped you from working out?

That's what makes incorporating exercise into your Miracle Morning such a game changer: it happens before you have an entire day to come up with excuses to avoid exercise and before your day wears you out and you're too tired. The Miracle Morning is a surefire way to make exercise a daily habit, which will enable you to perform at your physical, mental, and emotional best every single day.

Disclaimer: Hopefully this goes without saying, but you should consult your doctor or physician before beginning any exercise regimen, especially if you are experiencing physical pain, discomfort, disabilities, and similar. You may need to modify or even refrain from your exercise routine to meet your individual needs.

R Is for Reading

"Reading is to the mind what exercise is to the body and prayer is to the soul. We become the books we read."
—Matthew Kelly

"Today a reader, tomorrow a leader."
—Margaret Fuller

It has been said that experience is our greatest teacher. Whoever said that may have failed to clarify whether the experience must be our own or if our greatest teacher could also be gleaned from the experience had by others. If the latter is true, then that would help explain why the fifth practice in the S.A.V.E.R.S.—reading—is one of the most efficient and effective methods for acquiring the knowledge, perspectives, and strategies you need to change, improve, or optimize any area of your life.

To be clear, I'm referring to reading nonfiction content written by authors who have gotten results that are in alignment with those you aspire to, so you don't have to reinvent the wheel. You can achieve everything you want much faster by modeling someone who has already achieved it. With an almost infinite number of books available on nearly every topic, there are no limits to the knowledge you can gain through daily reading.

Want to be happier? Healthier? Wealthier? Are you looking to start a business, run a marathon, or be a better parent? There are countless books written by those who have already done these things and will teach you how you can do the same, thereby shortening your learning curve and accelerating your success.

How Long Should You Read For?

In the next two chapters, we'll explore various durations for each of your S.A.V.E.R.S, but I recommend dedicating at least 10 minutes of your Miracle Morning to reading, and longer if you'd prefer. Personally, I allocate 20 minutes of my Miracle Morning to reading (and I also read again for 10 to 20 minutes before bed). However, keeping in mind that it only takes *one* big idea to change your life, I encourage you to consider *quality over quantity* and *less is more* approaches to reading.

Let's do some quick math to help put into perspective how a relatively small amount of daily reading can make a profound impact in your life. Although reading speeds naturally vary from one person to the next, the average reader can get through around three hundred words in a minute. Most statistics consider a page to contain roughly three hundred words, so on average, reading a page takes roughly one minute, or two minutes if you're reading at a slower pace. Thus, 10 minutes of reading would result in an average of 5 to 10 pages read.

If you quantify that, reading just 10 pages a day will average 3,650 pages a year, which equates to about eighteen 200-page books. Let me ask you: If you read 18 personal or professional development books in the next 12 months, do you think you will be more knowledgeable, capable, and confident—a new and improved *you*? Absolutely! Reading 10 pages per day is not going to break you, but it will *make* you.

What Should You Read?

What you should read is determined by your goals. When people are surveyed and asked what they want more than anything, the number one answer is typically "happiness." I don't know about you, but I'm always striving to be happy and enjoy life, and here are some books that have helped me do that:

- *The Happiness Equation* by Neil Pasricha
- *The Happiness Advantage* by Shawn Anchor
- *The Art of Happiness* by the Dalai Lama
- *Loving What Is* by Byron Katie
- *The Untethered Soul*, *Living Untethered*, and *The Surrender Experiment* by Michael Singer

Another one of the most popular answers when asking people what they want is, not surprisingly, "more money." If you want to improve your financial situation, here are some of my favorite books, including the newest titles in the Miracle Morning book series:

- *Think and Grow Rich* by Napoleon Hill
- *Secrets of the Millionaire Mind* by T. Harv Eker
- *Total Money Makeover* by Dave Ramsey
- *The Miracle Morning for Entrepreneurs* coauthored by Cameron Herold, with Honorée Corder
- *Miracle Morning Millionaires* coauthored by David Osborn, with Honorée Corder

Want to create an incredibly loving, supportive, and harmonious romantic relationship? There are probably more books on how to do exactly that than you could read in a decade. Here are a few of my favorites:

- *The 5 Love Languages* by Gary Chapman
- *Choose Her Every Day* by Bryan Reeves
- *The Seven Principles for Making a Marriage Work* by John M. Gottman and Nan Silver
- *The Miracle Morning for Couples* coauthored by Lance and Brandy Salazar, with Honorée Corder (for couples who want to work on their relationship together)
- *The Miracle Morning for Transforming Your Relationship* coauthored by Stacey and Paul Martino, with Honorée Corder (for individuals who want to know how they can improve their relationship when their partner may not be on board)

Whether you want to be happier, make more money, transform your relationships, increase your self-confidence, be a better parent, or transform any other area of your life, visit your local bookstore or head to Amazon.com, and you'll find a plethora of books on any aspect of your life or yourself that you want to improve. For those who want to minimize your carbon footprint or save money, your local library is also a wonderful resource.

Tips to Maximize the Value of Your Reading

- **Begin with the end in mind.** Before you begin reading each day, ask yourself why you are reading that book. What do you want to gain from it? How will you implement what you're learning? Keep those outcomes in mind. I invite you take a moment to do this now by asking yourself what you want to gain from reading *this* book. More importantly, are you committed to implementing what you're learning by completing the Miracle Morning 30-Day Journey in Chapter 10?

- **Read religious texts.** Some Miracle Morning practitioners use their reading time to catch up on their religious texts, such as the Bible, Tanakh (the Hebrew Bible), Quran, or any other.
- **Mark up your books.** Hopefully, you took the suggestion I made in the beginning of this book, and you've been underlining, circling, highlighting, folding the corners of pages, and taking notes in the margins. To get the most out of any book I read and make it easy for me to revisit the content again in the future, I underline or circle anything that I may want to revisit, and I make notes in the margins to remind me why I underlined that particular section. This process of marking up books as I read allows me to come back at any time and recapture the key lessons, ideas, and benefits in a fraction of the time without needing to read the entire book again.
- **Reread books to master the content.** I highly recommend rereading useful personal development books. Rarely can we read a book once and internalize all the value contained within. Our first read merely exposes us to the ideas in the book. But achieving mastery requires repetition—exposing ourselves to specific ideas, strategies, and techniques repeatedly until they become ingrained in our subconscious and integrated into our life. Whenever I'm reading a book that I see will really make an impact on an area of my life, I commit to rereading that book (or at least the parts I've underlined, circled, and highlighted) as soon as I'm finished reading it the first time. I keep a special space on my bookshelf for the books that I want to reread and often refer to them throughout the year. Rereading requires discipline because it is typically more fun to read a book you've never read before.

Repetition can be boring or tedious (which is why so few people ever master anything), but that's even more reason why we should do it—to develop a higher level of self-discipline.

Why not try it out with this book? Commit to rereading it as soon as you're finished to deepen your learning and give yourself more time to master your mornings.

S Is for Scribing

"Whatever it is that you write, putting words on the page is a form of therapy that doesn't cost a dime."
—Diana Raab

"Ideas can come from anywhere and at any time. The problem with making mental notes is that the ink fades very rapidly."
—Rolf Smith

Scribing is the final practice in the Life S.A.V.E.R.S. and is just another word for *writing*. In full disclosure, I wouldn't normally use the word *scribing* in place of *writing*, but I needed an *S* for the end of Life S.A.V.E.R.S. because a *W* would have made it awkward. Thanks, thesaurus; I owe you one.

My favorite form of scribing is journaling, which I do for 5 to 10 minutes during my Miracle Morning. By getting our thoughts out of our head and putting them in writing, we gain valuable insights we might otherwise never see. The scribing element of your Miracle Morning enables you to document your insights, ideas, breakthroughs, realizations, successes, and lessons learned, as well as any areas of opportunity, personal growth, or improvement.

While I had known about the profound benefits of journaling for years—and I had even tried it a few times—I never stuck with it consistently because it was never part of my daily routine. Usually, I kept a journal by my bed, and when I'd get home late at night, 9 times out of 10, I would find myself making the excuse that I was too tired to write in it. My journals stayed mostly blank. Even though I already had many mostly blank journals sitting on my bookshelf, every so often I would buy myself a brand-new journal—a more expensive one—convincing myself that if I spent a lot of money on it, I would surely write in it. Seems like a decent theory, right? Unfortunately, my little strategy never worked, and I accumulated more and more increasingly expensive, yet equally empty, journals for years.

That was before the Miracle Morning. From day one, my Miracle Morning gave me the time and structure to write in my journal *every day*, and it quickly became one of my favorite habits. I can tell you now that journaling has become one of the most gratifying and fulfilling practices of my life. Not only do I derive the daily benefits of consciously directing my thoughts and recording them in writing, but I am able to go back and review my journals to relive meaningful experiences and gain powerful insights.

Gap Focus: Is It Hurting or Helping You?

In the opening pages of this chapter, we talked about using the Life S.A.V.E.R.S. to close your potential gap. Human beings are conditioned to have what I refer to as *gap focus*. We tend to focus on the gaps between where we are in life and where we want to be, the gaps between what we've accomplished and what we want to accomplish, and any perceived gaps between who we are and our idealistic vision of the person we believe we should be.

The problem with this is that constant gap focus can be detrimental to our confidence and self-image, causing us to feel like we don't have enough, haven't accomplished enough, and aren't good enough or, at least, not as good as we should be.

High achievers are typically the worst at this, constantly overlooking or minimizing their accomplishments, beating themselves up over every mistake and imperfection, and never feeling like anything they do is quite good enough.

The irony is that gap focus is a big part of the reason that high achievers *are* high achievers. Their insatiable desire to close the gap is what fuels their pursuit of excellence and constantly drives them to achieve. Gap focus can be healthy and productive if it comes from a positive, proactive "I'm committed to and excited about fulfilling my potential" perspective, without any feelings of lack. Unfortunately, it rarely does. The average person, even the average high achiever, tends to focus negatively on their gaps.

The highest achievers—those who are balanced and focused on achieving level 10 success in nearly every area of their lives—are exceedingly grateful for what they have, regularly acknowledge themselves for what they've accomplished, and are always at peace with where they are in their lives. It's a dueling idea: "I am doing the best that I can at this moment, and at the same time, I can and will do better." This balanced self-assessment prevents that feeling of lack—of not being, having, doing enough—while still allowing them to constantly strive to close their potential gap in each area.

Typically, when a day, week, month, or year ends and we're in gap-focus mode, it's almost impossible to maintain an accurate assessment of ourselves and our progress. For example, if you had 10 things on your to-do list for the day—even if you completed six of them—your gap focus causes you to feel that you didn't get everything done that you wanted to get done.

Most people do dozens, even hundreds, of things correctly and a few things wrong during the day. Guess which things people remember and replay in their minds over and over again? Doesn't it make more sense to focus on the hundreds of things you did right? Surely, it's more enjoyable.

What does this have to do with writing in a journal? Writing in a journal each day with a structured, strategic process allows you to direct your focus to what you did accomplish, what you're grateful for, and what you're committed to doing better tomorrow. This all helps you to enjoy your journey, feel good about forward progress, and access a heightened level of clarity to accelerate your results.

My First Journal Review

After my first year doing the Miracle Morning and writing in my journal each day, I discovered what I've found to be one of the most beneficial aspects of journaling: a journal review. The last week of the year, I went back and read every journal entry from that year. Day by day, I was able to review, remember, and *relive* my entire year. I was able to revisit my mindset each day and gain a new perspective as to how much I had grown throughout the year. I re-examined my actions, activities, and progress, gaining a new appreciation for how much I had accomplished during the past 12 months. Most importantly, I recaptured the lessons I had learned, many of which I had forgotten over the course of the year.

I also experienced what I call gratitude 2.0—a much deeper quality of gratitude than I had experienced before—on two different levels. It was what I now refer to as my first *Back to the Future* moment. Try to follow me here (and feel free to picture me as Marty McFly stepping out of a 1981 DeLorean). As I read through my journal, looking back at all the people, experiences, lessons, and accomplishments that I was grateful for throughout the year, I was reliving the gratitude that I felt in the past. At the same time, I was grateful in the present moment for how far I had come. It was a remarkable experience and a bit surreal. And I'm excited for you to experience it for yourself.

Then, I began to tap into the highest point of value I would gain from reviewing my journals: accelerated growth. I pulled out a sheet of blank paper, drew a line down the middle, and wrote two headings at the top: *Lessons Learned* and *New Commitments*. As I read through my journal entries, I found myself recapturing dozens of valuable lessons. This process of recapturing *lessons learned* and making *new commitments* to implement those lessons influenced my personal growth and development more than almost anything else. I owe much of my own progress to this one exercise.

Final Thoughts on the S.A.V.E.R.S.

Everything is difficult before it's easy. Every new habit is uncomfortable before it's comfortable. The more you practice the S.A.V.E.R.S., the more natural and normal each of them will feel. My first time meditating was almost my last. My mind raced, and my thoughts bounced around uncontrollably like the silver sphere in a pinball machine. But now, I love meditating. Similarly, my first time doing yoga, I felt like a fish out of water. I wasn't flexible, couldn't do the poses correctly, and felt awkward and uncomfortable. Now, yoga is my favorite form of exercise, and I'm so grateful that I stuck with it.

Here's some excellent advice from Miracle Morning practitioner Alaina Cash, especially if there's one or more S.A.V.E.R.S. you don't feel confident about: "Focus on sharpening one of the S.A.V.E.R.S. at a time. For example, if you're not confident in Silence, download an app, follow some YouTube videos, or ask for help in the Miracle Morning Community Facebook group and give Silence some extra attention for a week or until you feel confident in it. Do this while also getting the other S.A.V.E.R.S. done if you can. I've benefited from focusing on sharpening them one at a time each week and using more outside resources to help me become more confident in the practices. This helped me pivot from focusing more on the S.A.V.E.R.S. that were easier or more enjoyable to me to giving balance to all my S.A.V.E.R.S."

Consider this a tip from Christopher Moscarino, who shared in the opening pages how the Miracle Morning transformed his and his wife's financial situation: "Start small! Implement one to two S.A.V.E.R.S. at a time and maybe start with 5 minutes and work your way up. If the goal is to wake up an hour or more earlier than you have been, start with small increments—15 minutes, then 30, and so on. Start small, keep it simple, and before you know it you will be a consistent Miracle Morning practitioner."

In "Chapter 8: Customizing Your Miracle Morning," you'll learn how you can personalize nearly every aspect of your Miracle Morning. For now, here is an example of a fairly common (60-minute) Miracle Morning routine using the S.A.V.E.R.S.

- **S**ilence (10 minutes)
- **A**ffirmations (10 minutes)
- **V**isualization (5 minutes)
- **E**xercise (10 minutes)
- **R**eading (20 minutes)
- **S**cribing (5 minutes)

The order in which you do the S.A.V.E.R.S. can be adjusted. For example, some people prefer to exercise first to get their blood flowing and become more alert. However, you might prefer exercise as your last activity so you're not sweaty during the rest of your Miracle Morning. Personally, I prefer to start with a period of peaceful, purposeful silence so that I can wake up slowly, clear my mind, and optimize my mental and emotional state for the day.

I invite you to begin practicing the S.A.V.E.R.S. now, so you can become familiar and comfortable with each of them and get a jump start before you begin your 30-Day Life Transformation Journey in Chapter 10. If your biggest concern is still finding the time to fit this in, don't worry, I've got you covered. In the next chapter, you're going to learn how to do the entire Miracle Morning—receiving the full benefits from all six of the S.A.V.E.R.S.—in only six minutes a day.

7

THE 6-MINUTE MIRACLE MORNING

(For Those Days When You're Short on Time)

"On the one hand, we all want to be happy. On the other hand, we all know the things that make us happy. But we don't do those things. Why? Simple. We are too busy. Too busy doing what? Too busy trying to be happy."
—Matthew Kelly

"I don't have time to wake up early."
—Unknown

Oh, you're busy? Weird. I thought it was just me.

One of the most common concerns I hear from people new to the Miracle Morning is the idea of adding anything else to their already hectic life. Of course, adding the Miracle Morning makes life less hectic as you become more at peace, focused, productive, and capable of handling anything life throws at you. Still, there will always be some mornings when you simply don't have a full 30 to 60 minutes for your Miracle Morning.

Many of us tend to have an all-or-nothing mentality when it comes to how much time we believe we should take to do something. Early on, I found myself doing exactly that with my Miracle Mornings. If I didn't have the full hour that I wanted, I just skipped it. I realized this wasn't ideal. For one thing, doing anything related to personal development is almost always better than doing nothing. So, one morning, I had an early appointment, and after I got dressed, I only had 15 minutes until I needed to leave the house. I was about to skip my Miracle Morning when I thought, *What if I just did one minute for each of the S.A.V.E.R.S?*

I sat down on my couch, set the timer on my phone, and began my first six-minute Miracle Morning.

Imagine if the first six minutes of every morning began like this:

Minute 1: Silence

Instead of rushing carelessly into your hectic day—stressed and overwhelmed—you spend the first minute sitting quietly and enjoying a period of peaceful, purposeful silence. You sit, taking slow, deep breaths, with no one and nothing demanding your attention. Maybe you say a prayer of gratitude to appreciate the moment or pray for guidance on your journey. Maybe you enjoy a minute of meditation. As you sit in silence, you're totally present to this moment. You calm your mind, relax your body, and allow all your stress to melt away.

Minute 2: Affirmations

You pull out your Miracle Morning affirmations—the ones that clearly articulate and remind you of the exciting improvements you're committed to making in your life, the reasons they mean so much to you, and which actions you'll take to ensure that you achieve everything you want. You read them from top to bottom, and as you focus on what's most important to you, your level of internal motivation increases as you realize that, day by day, you are transforming your affirmations into your reality.

Minute 3: Visualization

You close your eyes and visualize what you need to do today to reach your goals. You visualize the day going perfectly, see yourself enjoying your work, smiling and laughing with your loved ones, and easily accomplishing all that you intend to accomplish for that day. You see what it will look like, you feel what it will feel like, and you experience the joy of what you will create. You rehearse being in a peak emotional state that you'll revisit at the appropriate times during the day. Seeing and feeling yourself showing up at your best reminds you of how capable you are and gives you a feeling of confidence.

Minute 4: Scribing

You write down one thing that you're grateful to have in your life, and then put your hand on your heart and feel a deep sense of gratitude. With 30 seconds to go, you optimize your productivity by clarifying, in writing, your top priority for the day to ensure you make progress toward a level 10 goal. In just 60 seconds of scribing, you've been able to enhance your emotional well-being and your productivity for the day.

Minute 5: Reading

Then, you open the book you've been reading, and in just one minute you're able to learn something useful that you can apply to your life. Maybe it's a new perspective that helps you see things in a new way. Or better yet, maybe you learn something tangible that you can incorporate into your day and that will improve your results at work or in your relationships. You feel empowered with this new-found knowledge that you can use to improve your life.

Minute 6: Exercise

Finally, you stand up and spend the last minute engaged in exercise, moving your body for 60 meaningful seconds. Maybe you run in place or do a minute of jumping jacks. Maybe you do push-ups or sit-ups. You may not break a sweat, but the point is that you're getting your heart rate up, generating energy, and increasing the flow of blood and oxygen to your brain, which increases your ability to be alert and focused.

How would you feel if that's how you utilized the first six minutes of each day? How would the quality of your day—your life—improve?

To be clear, I'm not suggesting that you limit your Miracle Mornings to only six minutes every day, as investing more time engaged in the S.A.V.E.R.S.—ideally 30 to 60 minutes—certainly deepens the impact of the practice. But on those days when you're pressed for time, the six-minute Miracle Morning still provides a powerful framework for accelerating your personal development and putting yourself in a peak physical, mental, and emotional state to optimize your day.

What's more, the six-minute Miracle Morning eliminates your "I don't have time" excuse and allows you to consistently practice the Miracle Morning. This consistency is critical to building the habit of daily practice.

8

CUSTOMIZING YOUR MIRACLE MORNING

"The Miracle Morning is amazing. It has provided new levels of clarity, focus, and energy to my life. What's great is that it can be a different routine for each person, depending on your goals and schedule. For me, as a business owner and mother of a one-year-old, it has been a time to reflect, pray, focus on my goals and dreams, exercise, and destress. It also gives me valuable time to be thankful for the people, events, and blessings in my life. We all have the same 168 hours in a week; start using the Miracle Morning, and you'll find miracles in your life that you never knew existed!"

—Katie Heaney (Saint Louis, Missouri)

Your Miracle Morning is 100 percent customizable. Everything from what time you wake up and which activities you do for each of your S.A.V.E.R.S. to how long you spend on each one is all up to you. There are no limits to how your Miracle Morning can be personalized to fit your lifestyle and help you achieve your most significant goals. In this chapter, I'll give you some ideas and strategies for how you can make this work for you. I'll also address when (and what) to eat in the morning, how to align your Miracle Morning with your major goals and dreams, what to do on the weekends, a tip on overcoming procrastination, and much more.

Plus, I'll include examples of different real-life Miracle Mornings, designed by individuals—from stay-at-home parents and entrepreneurs to high school and college students—to fit their unique schedules, priorities, and lifestyles.

Being Flexible with Your Miracle Morning and S.A.V.E.R.S.

This may sound completely counterintuitive but stick with me. You don't have to do the Miracle Morning *in the morning*.

Huh?

Of course, there are undeniable advantages to rising early and getting a proactive start to your day, which we have discussed at length. However, some readers have schedules and lifestyles that simply may not allow it. Obviously, someone who works the graveyard shift and sleeps during the day is going to have a different wake-up time than someone who is in bed by 9 PM every night.

Considering that different people have different schedules, it's important to remember that the essence of the Miracle Morning is waking up earlier than you *have to* and dedicating the *first part of your day* to personal development. If you drive a semitruck or work in a hospital from 10 PM to 6 AM and normally sleep until 2 PM, your Miracle Morning might start at 1:30 in the afternoon. What matters is that you begin your day with the S.A.V.E.R.S. so that you can start every day in a peak physical, mental, emotional, and spiritual state—no matter what time that might be.

Others might have a more fractured, unpredictable, or inconsistent schedule, such as an on-call doctor or nurse, or the parents of an infant. If that describes you and you've been feeling like this might not work for you, I've also got you covered. Consider that the S.A.V.E.R.S. represent six of the most timeless, proven personal development practices, whose benefits are *not* restricted to the morning.

I've seen new moms post in the Miracle Morning Community about how they break their S.A.V.E.R.S. up and do one or two at a time while their newborns are napping. I've also seen shift workers in New York City say they complete their S.A.V.E.R.S. while riding the subway to work. Finding a way to get it done is what matters, and there is always a way when you're committed.

Here's one such story from Molly Mathews, a mother of two who has been doing her Miracle Mornings consistently for a year:

I was introduced to the Miracle Morning about a year ago after several successful mentors highly recommended it. I began it as a stay-at-home mom of two young kids and was struggling day to day with getting things done, feeling burned out and exhausted. I started incorporating S.A.V.E.R.S. for just five minutes in each category, waking up just 30 to 40 minutes earlier than my kids, and I felt the shift almost immediately in how much smoother my day went. I started having more energy and more clarity and feeling like a better mom. My mental health and overall happiness improved drastically! I have since added more time to each of the S.A.V.E.R.S.; I don't always accomplish all of them before my kids are up for the day, but just taking some time for myself first thing makes a big difference. If I don't get in all of my S.A.V.E.R.S., first thing, then I still make sure to get them in during nap time. Now I run two businesses in my downtime, am a full-time mom and wife, and have so much more passion and excitement for life! I am so glad I found the Miracle Morning!

So, while beginning your day with the Miracle Morning may be ideal, committing to getting your S.A.V.E.R.S. done each day, regardless of the time, order, or duration—no matter what—is what will enable you to continuously grow, evolve, and become the person you need to be to create and experience everything you want for your life.

What About Weekends?

When I was doing research for this book, I came across a quote from Oprah Winfrey that I resonated with: "Waking up early on Saturday gives me an edge in finishing my work with a very relaxed state of mind. There is a feeling of time pressure on weekdays that isn't there on weekends. If I wake up early in the morning, before anybody else, I can plan the day or at least my activities with a relaxed mind." I couldn't agree more.

Like many newbies, when I first started doing Miracle Mornings, I did them only Monday through Friday, and I took the weekends off. It didn't take long for me to realize that every day I did my S.A.V.E.R.S., I felt better, more fulfilled, and more productive, and every day that I slept in, I usually woke feeling lethargic, unfocused, and unproductive.

Experiment for yourself. You may start, as I did, by doing the Miracle Morning during the week and taking the weekends off. See how you feel on those Saturday and Sunday mornings. If you feel, like many people do, that *every* day is better when you begin it with your Miracle Morning, you might just find that weekends are your favorite time to do it.

When, Why, and What to Eat in the Morning

Up until this point, you may have been wondering, *When do I get to eat breakfast in relation to my Miracle Morning?* Besides *when* you eat, *what* you choose to eat is even more critical, and *why* you choose to eat what you eat may be most important of all.

When to Eat

Keep in mind that digesting food is one of the most energy-draining processes that the body endures each day. The bigger the meal, the more food you are burdening your body with having to digest and the more drained you will feel. With that in mind, I recommend eating *after* your Miracle Morning. This ensures that, for optimum alertness and focus during the S.A.V.E.R.S., your blood will be flowing to your brain rather than to your stomach to digest your food.

If you feel like you must eat something first thing in the morning, make sure that it's a small, light, easily digestible meal, such as fresh fruit or a smoothie, and ideally includes healthy fat to fuel your brain (more on that in a minute).

Why to Eat

Let's take a moment to discuss *why* you eat the foods that you do. When you're shopping at the grocery store or selecting food from a menu at a restaurant, what criteria do you use to determine which foods you are going to put into your body? Are your choices based purely on taste? Texture? Convenience? Are they based on health? Energy? Longevity?

Most people eat the foods they do based mainly on the taste and, at a deeper level, their emotional attachment to the foods they like. If you were to ask someone, "Why did you eat that ice cream?" or "Why did you drink that soda?" or "Why did you bring that fried chicken home from the grocery store?" you would most likely hear responses like, "Mm, because I love ice cream!" or "I love the taste of soda!" or "I was in the mood for fried chicken!" All answers based on the emotional enjoyment derived primarily from the way these foods taste. In this case, this person is not likely to explain their food choices with regards to how much value these foods will add to their health or how much sustained energy they'll enjoy as a result.

My point is this: if you want to have more energy (we all do) and if you want your life to be healthy and disease-free (who doesn't?), then it is crucial that you re-examine why you eat the foods that you do and—this is important—start making a conscious choice to place significantly more value on the health and energy consequences (and benefits) of the foods you choose than you do on the taste. In no way am I saying that you should eat foods that don't taste good in exchange for health and energy benefits. I am saying that you can have both. If you want to live every day with an abundance of energy so you can perform at your best and live a long, healthy life, you must choose to eat more foods that contribute to your health and give you sustained energy, as well as taste great.

What to Eat (and Drink)

Before we talk about what to eat, let's take a second to talk about what to drink. Remember that step 4 of the five-step snooze-proof wake-up strategy (see page 57) is to drink a full glass of water—first thing in the morning—so you can rehydrate and re-energize after a full night of sleep. Extra points when you add a little sea salt and freshly squeezed lemon juice. Sea salt can help balance your potassium and sodium levels. This is actually an issue for many people, but they don't realize it. When dissolved in water, potassium and sodium turn into ions, which are essential for optimal neurological health, cardiovascular system function, and cellular health. Lemon juice helps to alkalize the body, which is beneficial to balancing the typically acid-heavy diet that the average person consumes.

As for what to eat, a diet rich in living foods, such as organic fruits and vegetables, as well as healthy fats for your brain, will greatly increase your energy levels, keep you healthy, protect you from disease, and improve your mental and emotional well-being.

After I drink a glass of water, the first thing I eat is a tablespoon of organic coconut oil, which is available at most health food stores. That provides my brain fuel to start the day and engage in my Miracle Morning and puts something in my stomach to take my vitamins with.

Around 7:30 AM, while I'm helping Ursula get our children ready for school, I make what I refer to as my Miracle Morning superfood smoothie. It is a low-sugar, nutrient-rich blend of healthy fats from organic pecans and chia seeds, immunity-boosting nutrition from organic berries and spinach, stimulating and mood-lifting phytonutrients from cacao nibs, and a boost of caffeine and polyphenols from organic matcha green tea, all topped off with an organic plant-based vanilla protein powder. I also regularly change up the ingredients to keep it interesting. You can get the most up-to-date recipe at MiracleMorning.com/resources. That way, you can keep the printed recipe by your blender and not your copy of this book. If you're like me, you might occasionally forget to secure the lid on your blender and end up with superfood smoothie all over your kitchen (true story). And that's definitely *not* a Miracle Morning!

Remember the old saying "you are what you eat"? Take care of your body so your body will take care of you. I recommend applying the 80/20 rule here—as long as 80 percent of your food choices are healthy, you can splurge a little on the other 20 percent. The way I do it is eating an organic plant-based diet for the first 10 to 12 hours that I'm awake (a smoothie for breakfast, salad for lunch, organic nuts for snacks in between), which provides my body and brain with an abundance of energy. Then for dinner, I'll usually have a small portion of high-quality meat, such as pasture-raised chicken, wild-caught fish, grass-fed beef, and so on, along with a serving of organic vegetables. Think of it as "vegan by day, paleo by night."

How to Use the S.A.V.E.R.S. to Achieve Your Goals and Dreams

Most of us have goals we want to achieve or changes we want to make, and Miracle Morning practitioners use their S.A.V.E.R.S. to enhance their ability to achieve their goals and make their desired changes. This is especially true of any goals they've been putting off or haven't been making time for—such as starting a business or writing a book. The S.A.V.E.R.S. will absolutely improve your ability to stay focused on your goals and identify which actions you need to take each day to make consistent forward progress.

For example, use some of your time spent in **silence** to contemplate your goals and embody the mental and emotional states that will help you achieve them.

When you create your **affirmations** using the results-oriented formula you learned earlier, make sure that you incorporate your most important goals and dreams so that your affirmations continually reinforce your clarity and commitment to follow through. Reading them daily will keep you focused on your highest priorities and the actions you need to take to achieve them.

When you are doing your morning **visualization**, imagine yourself effortlessly enjoying the process of achieving your goals (like I did while training for the ultramarathon) and keep a clear picture of what it will look like once achieved. Remember to maintain an optimal emotional state as you visualize, which will compel you to take the actions you've affirmed. The more vivid and compelling your vision is, the more effective it will be in increasing your desire and motivation to take the necessary steps toward your goals each day.

Exercise is a bit of an anomaly in this case (unless your goals are fitness related), but you can always listen to podcasts or audiobooks related to the goals you are working toward while you **exercise**. I have a friend who records herself reciting her affirmations and then listens to them while running on the treadmill.

When choosing which books and articles to read, select those that are in alignment with your goals to help accelerate how quickly you achieve them. If you want to improve your marriage or make more money, **reading** books on those topics will inevitably increase your chances of success. Remember, I started my Miracle Morning during the Great Recession when I was broke and in debt, and it was reading *Book Yourself Solid* by Michael Port that taught me the strategies I needed to get more clients and turn my financial situation around.

Finally, your **scribing** time can be completely focused on your goals. You can brainstorm the various ways you could reach your goals. You can clarify your top priorities in writing. You can acknowledge yourself for the progress you've made. You can reflect on your efforts and identify any areas where you may need to adjust your approach.

Whatever your goals—whether improving your marriage, increasing your income, losing weight, beating cancer, starting a blog, changing careers, becoming an entrepreneur, or any other meaningful outcome—your daily S.A.V.E.R.S. routine will help you to show up at your best every day so that you can achieve them.

Keeping Your Miracle Morning Fresh, Fun, and Exciting!

Over the last decade and a half, I estimate that I've done somewhere in the neighborhood of 4,500 Miracle Mornings. During that time, I've realized that my Miracle Morning will never stop evolving. While I still practice the S.A.V.E.R.S. every day and don't see any reason I would ever stop wanting to experience the benefits of those six practices, I do think it's important to mix things up and keep variety in your Miracle Morning so things don't get boring or stale.

For example, you might change your morning exercise routine monthly. You could try different guided or self-directed meditations. As I mentioned when discussing affirmations, as you continue to learn, grow, and elevate your consciousness, your affirmations should be updated to reflect whom you're becoming and your current goals. Naturally, the books you read will change as you complete each one, giving you something new to look forward to.

You can also adjust your Miracle Morning on the fly based on your changing schedule, circumstances, and priorities for the day. When I'm preparing for an upcoming keynote speech, I allocate my visualization to practice and rehearse my performance. When I'm traveling and staying in hotels, I adjust my Miracle Morning accordingly. For example, if I'm scheduled to give a late-night keynote or workshop at a conference, I move my wake-up and start time a little later. As I've been writing this book (my number one goal at the moment), my S.A.V.E.R.S. have been heavily focused on helping me to complete it.

As you can see, you can always design, customize, and evolve your Miracle Morning to fit *your* lifestyle.

Final Thoughts on Customizing Your Miracle Morning

Most humans have an innate need for variety. For most of us, it's important to keep our Miracle Mornings feeling fresh and new. I once complained to my mentor, Jesse, that my job as a sales rep was getting repetitive and boring. His response was, "Whose fault is it that it's boring? And whose responsibility is it to make it fun again?" This is a valuable lesson in personal responsibility that I've never forgotten. Whether it's our routines or our relationships, it's our responsibility to actively and continuously make them the way we want them to be.

9

FROM UNBEARABLE TO UNSTOPPABLE

The 3-Phase Strategy to Establish Any Habit (in 30 Days)

"Successful people aren't born that way. They become successful by establishing the habit of doing things unsuccessful people don't like to do. The successful people don't always like doing these things themselves; they just get on and do them."

—Don Marquis

"Motivation is what gets you started. Habit is what keeps you going."

—Jim Rohn

It's been said that our quality of life is created by the quality of our habits. If a person is living a happy, healthy, and generally successful life, then that person has the habits in place to create and sustain their levels of happiness, health, and success. On the other hand, if someone is not experiencing the levels of success they want, they likely haven't yet put the necessary habits in place to create the results they want. Instill the habits, and the results will follow.

I hope by this point in our journey through this book, you are eager to instill the Miracle Morning as a daily, lifelong habit to help you live the life you deserve. In this chapter, you'll learn a simple approach to establishing new habits, and in the following chapter, we'll walk through how to apply these techniques to your first Miracle Morning 30-Day Life Transformation Journey.

Considering that your habits largely determine your quality of life, there is arguably no single *skill* more important to learn and master than optimizing your habits. You must identify, implement, and maintain the habits necessary to create the results you want in your life while learning how to let go of any destructive habits that are holding you back from achieving your true potential.

Habits are behaviors that are repeated regularly and tend to occur unconsciously. Whether you realize it or not, your life has been and will continue to be shaped by your habits. If you don't control your habits, your habits will control you.

Unfortunately, if you're like the rest of us, you didn't learn how to optimize your habits when you were growing up. There was no Habits 101 class offered in school, though it would have been arguably the most valuable class we could have taken. So, we tend to not only enter adulthood with an arsenal of bad habits but also add to our arsenal as we get older. Thankfully, there are now countless articles and books on the important topics of habits, including bestsellers *Atomic Habits* by James Clear, *Tiny Habits* by B. J. Fogg, *High Performance Habits* by Brendon Burchard, and *Habit Stacking* by S. J. Scott.

But if we never learned how to implement and sustain positive habits, it's no wonder most of us fail at virtually every attempt to improve them, time and time again. Take New Year's resolutions, for example.

Habitual Failure: New Year's Resolutions

Every year, millions of well-intentioned people make New Year's resolutions (NYRs), but few of us stick to them. An NYR is a *positive* habit (like exercising or early rising) that you want to incorporate into your life, or a *negative* habit (like smoking or eating fast food) that you want to get rid of. You don't need a statistic to tell you that when it comes to NYRs, most people have already given up and thrown in the towel before January ends.

Maybe you've seen this phenomenon in real time. If you've ever gone to the gym the first week of January, you know how difficult it can be to find a parking spot. The gym is packed with people who are armed with an NYR to lose weight and get in shape. However, if you go back to the gym closer to the end of the month, you'll notice that half of the parking lot is empty. Without a proven strategy to stick with their new habits, most people give up.

Why is it so difficult to implement and sustain the habits we need to be happy, healthy, and successful? For one, we are, at some level, addicted to our habits. Whether psychologically or physically, once a habit has been reinforced through enough repetition, it can be very difficult to change. Here are three common reasons people fail to create and sustain new habits:

- They don't know how long it's going to take to form their new habit, and without a predetermined time frame, it feels like it might take forever. I mean, who has that kind of time?
- They don't have clear expectations as to what the process is going to be like, so they're deterred by any physical or psychological discomfort or any unexpected challenges that arise.
- They don't have a simple and effective strategy to follow that will help ensure their success.

In other words, if you don't have an effective, proven strategy, you are more likely to fail in making a habit. Let's address and handle all of these pitfalls.

How Long Does It *Really* Take to Form a New Habit?

Depending on the book or article you read, or which expert you listen to, you'll hear compelling evidence that it takes anywhere from a single hypnosis session to three months to successfully incorporate a new habit into your life or to get rid of an existing one.

One popular philosophy, which may have originated in the 1960 book *Psycho-Cybernetics: A New Way to Get More Living Out of Life* by Dr. Maxwell Maltz, states that it takes 21 days to establish a new habit. Dr. Maltz found that amputees took, on average, 21 days to adjust to the loss of a limb. He also argued that it takes people 21 days to adjust to any major life changes.

Other philosophies are not so set on the number of days it takes for a habit to become automatic but instead emphasize that it also depends on how difficult the habit is. My personal experience, coupled with the real-world results I've seen working with hundreds of coaching clients and thousands of Miracle Morning practitioners, has led me to the conclusion that you can change any habit in 30 days (or less) if you have the right strategy. The problem is that most people don't have any strategy, let alone the right one. So, year after year, they lose confidence in themselves and their ability to improve as failed attempt after failed attempt piles up and knocks them down.

How can *you* become a master of your habits? How can you take complete control of your life—and your future—by learning how to identify, implement, and sustain any positive habit you want and permanently remove any negative habits? You're about to learn the *right* strategy, one most people know nothing about.

The Miracle Morning 3-Phase, 30-Day Habit Strategy

When you don't know what to expect and aren't prepared to overcome the mental and emotional challenges that are part of the process of implementing a new habit, it's easy to fail. This strategy remedies that.

We'll start by dividing the 30-day time frame into three 10-day phases. Each of these phases presents a different set of emotional challenges and mental roadblocks to sticking with the new habit, whether you are starting a positive one or ending a negative one. Since the average person doesn't realize these pitfalls are normal and expected, they think something is wrong and give up because they don't feel good and they don't know what to do to overcome them. You'll know better.

Phase 1: Unbearable (Days 1 to 10)
The first 10 days of implementing any new habit, or ridding yourself of any old habit, can feel almost unbearable. Although the first

few days can be easy and even exciting—because it's something *new*—as soon as the newness wears off, reality sets in. You hate it. It's painful. It's not fun anymore. Every fiber of your being tends to resist and reject the change. Your mind tells you: *I hate this.* Your body cries out: *I don't like how this feels.*

If your new habit is waking up early (which might be a useful one to get started on, now), the first 10 days might be something like this: [The alarm clock sounds.] *Oh God, it's morning already! I don't want to get up. I'm soooo tired. I need more sleep. Okay, just 10 more minutes.* [Hit snooze button.]

The problem for most people is that they don't realize that this seemingly unbearable first 10 days is only temporary. Instead, they think it's the way the new habit feels, and will always feel, telling themselves, *If the new habit is this painful, forget it—it's not worth it.*

As a result, too many of us have struggled, time and time again, to start exercise routines, quit smoking, improve our diets, stick to a budget, or any other habit that would improve our quality of life because all these new habits feel bad in the beginning. But this does not have to be the case for you.

When you are *prepared* for these first 10 days, when you know that it is the price you pay for success, when you know that the first 10 days will be challenging but they're also *temporary*, you can beat the odds and succeed! If the benefits are great enough, we can do anything for 10 days, right?

So, the first 10 days of implementing any new habit aren't a picnic. You'll defy it. You might even hate it at times. But you *can* do it. Especially considering that it only gets easier from here and the reward is, oh—just the ability to create *everything* you want for your life. If you anticipate the initial discomfort, you'll be able to ride it out to your desired goal.

Phase 2: Uncomfortable (Days 11 to 20)

After you get through the first 10 days—the most difficult 10 days—you begin the second 10-day phase, which is considerably easier. You will be getting used to your new habit. You will also have developed some confidence and positive associations with the benefits of your habit.

While days 11 through 20 are not unbearable, they are still uncomfortable and will require discipline and commitment on your part. At this stage, it will still be tempting to fall back to your old behaviors. If waking up early is your new habit, for example, it will still be easier to sleep in because you've done it for so long. Stay committed. You've already gone from *unbearable* to *uncomfortable*, and you're about to find out what it feels like to elevate yourself to being *unstoppable*.

Phase 3: Unstoppable (Days 21 to 30)

When entering the final 10 days—the home stretch—the few people who make it this far almost always make a detrimental mistake: adhering to the popular philosophy that it takes only 21 days to form a new habit.

The experts who support this claim are partly correct. It does take 21 days—the first two phases—to *form* a new habit. But the third 10-day phase is crucial to *sustaining* your new habit in the long term. The final 10 days is where you positively reinforce and associate pleasure with your new habit. Up until this point, you've been primarily associating pain and discomfort with it. This is where you turn that mindset around and start feeling proud of yourself for making it this far.

Phase 3 is also where the actual transformation occurs, as your new habit becomes part of your identity. It transcends the space between *something you're trying* and *who you're becoming*. You start to see yourself as someone who *lives* the habit.

For example, if you go from having an identity that says, "I am *not* a morning person" to "I *am* a morning person," instead of dreading your alarm clock in the morning, you are excited to wake up and get going when the alarm sounds because you've done it for over 20 days in a row. You're starting to see and feel the benefits.

Too many people get overly confident, pat themselves on the back, and think, *I've done it for 20 days so I'm just going to take a few days off.* The problem is that those first 20 days are the most challenging part of the process. Taking a few days off before you've invested the necessary time into positively reinforcing the habit makes it difficult to get back on track. It's days 21 through 30 where you start to experience exponential benefits and even begin to enjoy the habit, which is what will make it easier for you to continue it in the future.

Overcoming Our Self-Imposed Limitations

Remember my story from the beginning of this book, when my dear friend Jon Berghoff suggested I go for a run to help with my depression and gain the clarity I needed to solve my financial problems? And I told him, "I'm not a runner. In fact, I hate running. There's no way I could do it." Here's how my journey from not believing I was a runner to completing a 52-mile ultramarathon unfolded.

Roughly six months after I began practicing the Miracle Morning, Jon invited me to run the Atlantic City Marathon to raise money for the Front Row Foundation, a charity that we both sat on the board of. He stressed that I could run (or jog) any distance and joked that I could even walk a 5K with his grandma. He also explained to me that, at one time, he didn't believe he could run a marathon, but day by day, step by step, he developed himself into a runner. Eventually Jon ran not one but three ultramarathons, including a double-ultra, which was one hundred consecutive miles. "Come on, Hal," he joked, "if I can run a hundred miles, you can definitely run 26!" Somehow that logic didn't quite convince me.

"Yeah, I'll think about it," I said as a way to delay having to tell him *no*.

Don't get me wrong, I absolutely believed in and supported the life-changing work done by the Front Row Foundation. I had been donating a percentage of my income to the organization ever since it was founded by another one of my dear friends, Jon Vroman. But writing a check was a lot easier than running a marathon. Unless I was being chased, I hadn't intentionally run so much as a block in the 10 years since I graduated high school. And even back then, I only ran to keep from failing PE class.

Not to mention, ever since breaking my femur and pelvis in the car accident when I was 20, I always had a fear in the back of mind of what could happen if I put too much pressure on my leg. Every time I went snow skiing, I would have visions of taking a hard fall and then seeing the titanium rod in my leg break through the skin of my thigh. I know it's a gruesome image, but breaking your limbs, having them repaired with screws and rods, and then being told you're never going to walk again can do that to you.

Coincidentally, just a week after my conversation with Jon, one of my coaching clients, Katie Fingerhut, completed her second marathon. After we celebrated her accomplishment, I told her that I was considering it. "Hal, it's so amazing," she told me. "I feel like I can do anything now! You should definitely do it!"

After listening to Jon and Katie's enthusiastic testimonies for marathon running, I was starting to think maybe it was time for me to overcome my self-limiting belief about not being a runner. If they could do it, then so could I. I also considered that running a marathon would definitely force me to evolve toward a level 10 version of myself. That got me excited. So, I committed to start running.

The next morning, I decided to assess my physical capabilities and see just how far I could run. I used my Miracle Morning to support this, focusing my *Silence* on acclimating my nervous system to the idea of running, my *Affirmations* on reinforcing the perspective that I could become a runner, and my *Visualization* on seeing myself going for a run while in a peak emotional state. As soon as I completed the S, A, and V of my Miracle Morning, I laced up my Nike Air Jordan basketball shoes (I didn't even own running shoes) and headed out the front door of my house. The weird thing was that, thanks to the benefits of using my morning practices to prepare and optimize my mindset, I was actually looking forward to it!

I hustled out the front door of my house and down the driveway, feeling motivated and inspired. I took some deep breaths and increased my speed as I reached the sidewalk. *This isn't so bad,* I thought. *I'm going to become a runner!* And then, suddenly, as soon as I stepped off of the sidewalk and onto the street, I twisted my ankle and fell to the ground. *You've got to be kidding me.* I was now lying on the pavement, writhing in pain.

Thankfully, after a few minutes, I determined that it was only a minor sprain. I carefully made my way back to my feet and began limping toward my house, feeling disappointed, a little relieved that I didn't have to run, and mostly determined to try again. My life experiences had taught me that when we commit to something, the universe (or God) will usually test us to see how committed we really are. I thought to myself, *I'll try again tomorrow.* I was committed.

30 Days: "From Unbearable to Unstoppable" in Action

The next day, my ankle felt fine and I officially began my marathon training. But still, I only made it a few blocks before I was short on breath and reminded of what I believed for so long: *I am not a runner.* My hips ached. My previously broken femur was sore. I didn't have the stamina to run a mile, let alone 26 of them. I realized I needed help—I needed a plan. I went on Amazon.com and purchased the perfect book: *The Non-Runner's Marathon Trainer* by David Whitsett. Now I had a plan.

Days 1 to 10

The first 10 days of running were both physically painful and mentally challenging. Every single day, I fought a constant battle in my head with the voice of mediocrity, which told me it was okay to quit and that I didn't have to do this. But I knew that giving up was the easy thing, and only following through with my commitment—the right thing—would enable me to become a better version of myself. *Do the right thing, not the easy thing*, I reminded myself. I kept running. I was committed.

Days 11 to 20

Days 11 to 20 were only slightly less difficult. I still told myself that I didn't *like* running, but I didn't really *hate* it anymore. For the first time in my life, I was establishing the habit of running every day. It was no longer this scary, foreign experience that I watched other people doing on the sidewalk, while I was driving my car. After a few weeks of daily running, it was becoming normal for me to wake up and go for a run. I remained committed, and going for a run became increasingly easier.

Days 21 to 30

Days 21 to 30 were almost enjoyable, and I was gradually forgetting what it felt like to hate running. Since it was becoming a habit, I was doing it without much conscious thought or effort. I just woke up, put on my running shoes (yes, I had invested in a pair by then), and logged my miles each day. The mental battle was gone, replaced with reciting positive affirmations or listening to personal and professional development audios while I ran. In just 30 days, I had completely overcome my limiting belief that I couldn't run, and I had become what I have never imagined I could be . . . a runner. This also got me feeling confident in my abilities and considering what other limiting beliefs I could overcome and meaningful habits I could change in just 30 days.

The Rest of the Story: "52 Miles to Freedom"

After just four weeks of following my marathon training plan, in which I gradually increased the distance I ran each day, I had completed 50 miles, including a six-mile run! I called Jon to celebrate. He was excited for me, but never one to allow a friend to rest on their laurels, he presented me with a new challenge: "Hal, why don't you run an ultramarathon? If you're going to run 26 miles, you might as well run 52." Only Jon would suggest such logic.

"Hmm, that's an interesting idea. Let me give it some thought," I told him.

This time, when I told Jon I would think about it, I meant it. I was intrigued by the idea of pushing myself even farther and running 52 consecutive miles. The fact that I had been able to run 50 miles in a month, culminating in a six-consecutive-mile run, was shattering limitations I previously thought were true. Maybe Jon was right. If I could train to run 26 miles, I might as well train to run 52. I still had six months until the Atlantic City Marathon, so why not set the bar a little higher and go for 52? So, I did. I was even somehow able to convince a friend and two of my brave coaching clients to do it with me!

Six months later, I had logged 475 miles, including three 20-mile runs, and had traveled across the country to meet with two of my favorite coaching clients, James Hill and Favian Valencia, and longtime friend Alicia Anderer, so the four of us could attempt to run 52 miles together. Jon even flew out to show his support. There was just one logistical challenge: the Atlantic City Marathon course was 26.2 miles and wasn't set up for ultramarathon runners. So, we improvised.

We met on the boardwalk at 3:30 AM. Our goal was to finish our first 26 miles before the official marathon began at 8 AM, and then complete the second half with the regular marathon runners. The moment was surreal. The energy between the four of us was a blend of excitement, fear, adrenaline, and disbelief. Were we *really* going to do this?!

We might have been able to see our breath in the chilly October air had the moonlight been brighter. Nevertheless, our path was lit well enough, and so we began. One foot in front of the other, one step at a time, we moved forward. We all agreed that was the key to our success that day—keep moving forward. So long as we didn't stop putting one foot in front of the other, as long as we kept moving forward, we would eventually reach our destination.

Six hours and five minutes later, largely due to the collective support and accountability of our group working together as one unit, we completed our first 26 miles. This was a defining moment for each of us. Not because of the 26 miles we had behind us but because of the mental fortitude it was going to take to get ourselves to run the 26 miles we had ahead of us.

The excitement that permeated every fiber of our beings six hours earlier had been replaced with excruciating pain, fatigue, and mental exhaustion. Considering the physical and mental state we were in, we didn't know if we had it in us to duplicate what we had just done. Still, we pushed on.

A total of 15.5 hours from the time we started, James, Favian, Alicia, and I completed our 52-mile quest . . . together. One foot in front of the other, and one step at a time, we ran, jogged, walked, limped, and literally crawled across the finish line.

On the other side of that line was *freedom*—the kind of freedom that can never be taken away from you. It was freedom from our self-imposed limitations. Although through our training we had grown to believe that running 52 consecutive miles was *possible*, none of us really believed in our heart of hearts that it was probable, let alone inevitable. As individuals, each of us struggled with our own fears and self-doubt. But the moment we crossed that finish line, we had given ourselves the gift of freedom from our fears, our self-doubt, and our self-imposed limitations.

It was in that moment I realized that this is a gift of freedom not reserved for the chosen few, but one that is available to each and every one of us the moment we make the choice to take on challenges that are out of our comfort zone, forcing us to grow, to expand our capacity, to be and do more than we have been and done in the past. This is true freedom.

Are You Ready for True Freedom?

In the next chapter, the Miracle Morning 30-Day Life Transformation Journey will enable you to overcome your own self-imposed limitations so you can be, do, and have everything you want in your life faster than you ever thought possible. That is *true* freedom—the freedom to be, do, and have what you decide to create for yourself. The S.A.V.E.R.S. combine six life-changing daily habits into one ritual, and although most people who try it love it from day one, getting yourself to follow through with it for 30 days—so you can make it a lifelong habit—will require an unwavering commitment from you. On the other side of the next 30 days is you—becoming the person you need to be to create everything you've ever wanted for your life. What could be more exciting than that?

10

THE MIRACLE MORNING 30-DAY LIFE TRANSFORMATION JOURNEY

"An extraordinary life is all about daily, continuous improvements in the areas that matter most."
—**Robin Sharma**

"Life begins at the end of your comfort zone."
—**Neale Donald Walsh**

Let's play devil's advocate for a moment. Can the Miracle Morning really transform your life in just 30 days? I mean, come on, can anything really make *that* significant of an impact on your quality of life that quickly? Well, consider that it did for me, even when I was broke, depressed, and at my lowest point. It has for millions of people around the world. These are ordinary people, just like you and me, realizing we have it within us to become extraordinary.

Remember Keith Minick, whose son died just three hours after being born. Keith spent over a year suffering from depression and feeling dissatisfied with his career. Then, during his very first Miracle Morning, his mindset completely changed: "I set my alarm, got up, and began the S.A.V.E.R.S. I experienced instant changes in my psychology, physiology, and mental health. I took ownership of where I was and set forward a path and a process to achieve the life I wanted."

He went on to say, "I have been practicing the Miracle Morning routine for nearly a decade. The S.A.V.E.R.S. framework continues to be a major part of my life. A major factor to my success has been implementing, maintaining, and evolving my routine. I encourage anyone looking for a breakthrough, struggling with depression, or trying to get unstuck in life to read and implement the Miracle Morning S.A.V.E.R.S. framework."

Keith's story is a real-life example of just how fast things can change for you and how, 10 years later, you can still be evolving into the best version of yourself.

In the last chapter, you learned a simple, effective three-phase strategy for successfully implementing and sustaining any new habit in 30 days. We're now going to apply that strategy directly to the Miracle Morning practice with the Miracle Morning 30-Day Life Transformation Journey so that it feels like a seamless transition in your life.

In previous editions of this book, I referred to this as the 30-Day Life Transformation "Challenge." However, when writing this new edition, I realized that most of us already have more than enough challenges in our lives, and the Miracle Morning is really a journey of elevating your consciousness and becoming the best version of yourself. This chapter and the actions it lays out for you represent the first 30 days in your lifelong Miracle Morning journey.

In addition to the S.A.V.E.R.S., you'll identify other habits that you believe will have the most significant impact on your life, your success, who you want to be, and where you want to go. Then, you'll use the next 30 days to begin forming these habits, which will completely transform the *direction* of your life. By changing the direction of your life, you immediately change your quality of life—and, ultimately, you change where you end up.

Consider the Rewards

When you commit to the 30-Day Life Transformation Journey, you are committing to building a foundation for fulfilling your potential in every area of your life. You will begin each day with newfound levels of *clarity* (the power you'll generate from focusing on what's most important), *discipline* (the crucial ability to get yourself to follow through with your commitments), and *personal development* (perhaps the single most significant determining factor in your success). By waking up for your Miracle Morning and implementing your S.A.V.E.R.S. for the next 30 days, you'll find yourself quickly becoming the person you need to be to create and sustain the improvements you want to make now and for the rest of your life.

You'll also be transforming the Miracle Morning from a concept that you may be excited (and possibly a little intimidated) to implement into a lifelong habit that you'll be able to use to continue developing yourself into the person you need to be to continue creating the life you've always wanted. Even within these first 30 days, you'll experience profound improvements in your mindset and the way you feel.

By practicing the S.A.V.E.R.S. each day, you'll be experiencing the combined physical, intellectual, emotional, and spiritual benefits of silence, affirmations, visualization, exercise, reading, and scribing. Don't be surprised if you feel less stressed, more centered, more focused, happier, and more excited about your life.

If right now you're feeling hesitant or concerned about whether you will be able to follow through with this for 30 days, relax—it's completely normal to feel that way. This is especially true if waking up in the morning is something you've found challenging in the past. Remember, we all suffer from rearview mirror syndrome. So, it's expected that you will be a bit hesitant or nervous, and it's a sign that you're ready to commit. Otherwise, you wouldn't be nervous.

Remember, your life situation will improve after—but only *after*—you develop yourself into the person you need to be to improve it. That's exactly what these next 30 days of your life can be—a new beginning, and a new you.

3 Steps to Begin Your Miracle Morning 30-Day Life Transformation Journey

Step 1: Get the Miracle Morning 30-Day Life Transformation Kit

Visit MiracleMorning.com/resources to download, print, and begin filling out your free Miracle Morning 30-Day Journey Life Transformation Kit, which gives you exercises, affirmations, daily checklists, tracking sheets, and everything else you need to make starting and completing the 30-Day Life Transformation as easy as possible. This document will help you identify which area(s) of your life you want to improve, consider any obstacles you may need to overcome, clarify which actions you'll take to do so, and then align your daily Miracle Morning practice to help you follow through, similar to how I used the S.A.V.E.R.S. to double my income during the 2008 recession. Like anything in life that's worthwhile, successfully completing the 30-Day Life Transformation requires a bit of preparation, so it's important that you do the initial exercises in your Life Transformation Kit (which shouldn't take you more than 30 to 60 minutes). You can even do them during your *Scribing* time during your first Miracle Morning.

Step 2: Schedule Your First Miracle Morning for Tomorrow

Commit to and schedule your first Miracle Morning for tomorrow (yes, write it into your schedule) and decide where you will do it. Remember, I recommend that you leave your bedroom and remove yourself from the temptations of your bed altogether. My Miracle Morning takes place every day on my living room couch while everyone else in my house is still sound asleep. I've heard from people who enjoy doing their Miracle Morning outside in nature when the weather is nice. Do yours where you feel most comfortable but also where you won't be interrupted. Lastly, remember that this is about progress, not perfection! You don't even have to do all of the S.A.V.E.R.S. to start. As I mentioned in the last paragraph, you can begin with *Scribing* and continue filling out your Fast Start Kit. Or you can focus on *Reading* and continue with the two brand-new chapters that follow this one. What's most important is that you start your day with personal development, whether that's one of the S.A.V.E.R.S., all of them, or somewhere in between.

Step 3: Set Your Alarm and Move It Across the Room
As my first coach, Jeff Sooey, used to say, "This is where the rubber meets the road." Commit to waking up earlier (ideally 30 to 60 minutes before you *have to*) and doing your first Miracle Morning. It's not a must that you keep your alarm clock across the room, but you may remember from Chapter 5 that it forces you to get out of bed, and being upright makes it much easier to stay awake than when you're able to reach over to your nightstand to turn it off.

There's also an optional Step 4: download the free Miracle Morning Routine app. If you don't like using apps, you can disregard this step. But if you do like apps, this app provides you with added accountability by enabling you to track your progress each day and check your S.A.V.E.R.S. off as you complete each one. The additional resources include customizable timers, an affirmations creator, a built-in journal, and optional guided S.A.V.E.R.S. tracks so that you can complete your Miracle Morning by clicking "play" and following along. If you like using apps, this is a great free resource to help set yourself up for success.

Are You Ready to Transform Your Life?

Remember that when measuring our levels of success and fulfillment on a scale of 1 to 10, we were all born with an innate drive and desire to become the best version of ourselves and experience life at a level 10. What might taking the first steps in that direction look like for you? What are the next levels of success and fulfillment in your personal or professional life? Which abilities or habits do you need to develop to reach those levels?

No matter what your past has been, you *can* change your future by changing what you do in the present. Give yourself the gift of investing just 30 days to make significant improvements in your thoughts, words, and actions, thereby elevating your consciousness one morning at a time.

Pause.

Take a breath.

It's time to start living what you've been learning!

I've said throughout this book that reading is an incredibly valuable tool for personal transformation . . . *if* you convert what you learn into action. It's time to begin your daily Miracle Morning practice, if you haven't already.

There are two more chapters ahead that will help you to optimize your sleep and elevate your consciousness to a state of Inner Freedom. But these are best pursued once your Miracle Morning practice is underway. I recommend consuming these chapters during the "R" (reading) component of your S.A.V.E.R.S.

If, at any time, you want to revisit the steps to get started, go back and review "Chapter 10: The Miracle Morning 30-Day Life Transformation Journey." I'm so excited for you and the insights and growth you will experience! Good luck!

11

THE MIRACLE EVENING

Your Strategy for Blissful Bedtime and Better Sleep

"If you're going to bed at the same time and waking up at the same time each day, you will find that not only will the quality of your sleep improve, but in some cases, you might not need as much."
—Dr. Michael Breus, clinical psychologist and sleep medicine expert

"May the angels from heaven bring the sweetest of all dreams for you. May you have long and blissful sleep. Good night my friend!"
—Unknown

For years, people have asked what my evening ritual is. And, for years, I've been slightly embarrassed to tell them that I didn't have one. My answer always seemed to be a letdown. That was until I realized that being intentional about how we end our day might be as important as how we begin it. This chapter will help you to create your Miracle Evening ritual with the following benefits in mind:

- Overcoming difficulties falling and/or staying asleep.
- Letting go of stressful thoughts and feelings so you can go to bed feeling calm and relaxed.
- Setting up your internal and external environments to wake up feeling more refreshed and energized.
- Drifting off to sleep feeling grateful and at peace.

If you struggle with feeling stressed at the end of the day and have difficulties falling or staying asleep, this chapter is especially for you. As someone who has struggled with and overcome chronic insomnia and extended bouts of sleep deprivation, I know how physically, mentally, and emotionally devastating it can be. So, I am committed to doing whatever I can to help people end their days in a way that enables them to feel great and sleep well.

As I mentioned in Chapter 5, our mental and emotional state in the morning is typically a reflection of whatever mental and emotional state we dwell on as we fall asleep. What you allow yourself to focus on before bed can not only make it difficult to doze off, but also weighs on your subconscious mind while you sleep and affects how you feel when you wake up. So, if you end your day allowing yourself to think stressful thoughts, it will affect your ability to get a good night's sleep and you'll likely wake up feeling stressed and not feeling well-rested.

If, instead, you establish an evening routine that enables you to let go of stressful thoughts, calm your body and mind, and focus on what you're grateful for, then you're much more likely to fall asleep feeling peaceful, grateful, and happy, sleep well, and then wake up in that same blissful state. With this perspective in mind, it would only make sense to be highly intentional about how we close out each day to prepare our mind and body for not only restorative sleep but also an optimal start to the following day.

"I Want to Die"

From November 2019 to May 2020, I averaged two to four hours of sleep per night. If you've ever experienced even a single night when you were only able to sleep for a few hours, you know how detrimental that can be to your mental, emotional, and physical well-being. Six months of chronic sleep deprivation left me severely traumatized, experiencing hallucinations and thinking people were trying to kill me, suffering from unyielding depression and debilitating anxiety, and even contemplating suicide.

Each night, I would lay awake, tossing and turning and staring at the ceiling. My mind would race, plagued with all the crazy things going on in the world, problems in my personal life, and fear of my cancer coming back—all creating a storm of anxiety. My heart raced in unison with my mind, and cortisol flooded my veins, causing me to feel wide awake while simultaneously mentally and physically exhausted. During the day, I felt unwell and unhappy and spent much of my time in a very dark place.

The sleep deprivation was feeding my depression and anxiety, while depression and anxiety were contributing to my sleep deprivation. I was in a vicious cycle that would not end unless I did something to escape it. One night, from our guest bedroom, where I had been sleeping alone for the last two months so I wouldn't be disturbed when Ursula came to bed, I desperately sent her the following text message:

> *Sweetheart, I don't want to worry you, but I have to be honest. I want to die. I can't take this anymore, and I don't know what to do.*

A few hours later, Ursula woke up, read my text, and came into the guest room. She hugged me and told me she loved me. She was coming from a place of hopelessness as much as she was from a place of compassion. In full transparency, our marriage had barely survived the past few years and was on the verge of falling apart after the past six months. We were both suffering, but only I was the cause. Having not gotten a good night's sleep in nearly half a year, I had become a different person. I was not the positive, happy, joyful man that Ursula married. I was anxious, fearful, depressed, and unpleasant to be around. As much as she loved me, she could only take so much, and seeing me give up hope was causing her to do the same.

I began researching and experimenting with various strategies to improve my sleep. Similar to how the S.A.V.E.R.S. emerged in 2008 out of desperation and depression, the solution to my sleep nightmare came, over time, through trial and error, as I developed the Miracle Evening.

Around that time, I was scrolling through the Miracle Morning Community Facebook group when one of Brian Marshall's posts caught my eye. Brian has become one of the most consistent Miracle Morning practitioners in the world, having now completed over 2,200 consecutive Miracle Mornings (and counting) without ever missing a single day. According to Brian, he owes his uninterrupted track record of Miracle Mornings to the evening routine that set him up for success in the mornings, which he called R.E.S.T.E.R.S.—his own acronym to optimize bedtime and sleep. Brian's post that day read:

> I have recently completed more than 260 consecutive days of TMM. No breaks, no shorts, no missed days. My life has transformed into something far more enjoyable and deliberate. I feel vibrant and absolutely glowing with AWESOME. I am solidly behind the wheel of my life and have amazing clarity of purpose and direction. Each day I wake better than I was the day before because each day, I faithfully complete my S.A.V.E.R.S. My uninterrupted track record, however, is owing to an evening routine that I have also done for as many days. It's like S.A.V.E.R.S. in the evening. I have started to call them R.E.S.T.E.R.S.

The R.E.S.T.E.R.S. acronym stands for *Read, Exercise, Shower, Tally, Empower, Relax,* and *Sleep.* Like the S.A.V.E.R.S., Brian's R.E.S.T.E.R.S. provided simple, actionable steps to wind down in the evening and prepare the mind and body for optimal sleep, and inspired me to design the Miracle Evening ritual. My version includes some additional steps that I've found to be highly beneficial to prepare my physical, mental, and emotional state for an optimal night of sleep. There are also aspects of Brian's routine, such as showering, that I do every night automatically, so I didn't feel the need to include them in my written evening ritual.

I've organized the exact steps of the Miracle Evening into the acronym S.L.U.M.B.E.R.S. (I know, I know—so many acronyms). The word slumber is defined as "to sleep," and since the ultimate objective of this routine is to help you sleep better, it felt like an appropriate acronym. I'll walk you through each of the steps and then give you some thoughts on how you can use them as is or as a springboard to design your own Miracle Evening.

The S.L.U.M.B.E.R.S.

My Miracle Evening starts a few hours before bedtime and has enabled me to go from being a sufferer of chronic insomnia and sleep deprivation to sleeping peacefully and waking up feeling refreshed and rejuvenated. My current Miracle Evening can be summarized into the following steps:

- **S**top eating three to four hours before bed.
- **L**et go of stressful thoughts and feelings.
- **U**se natural sleep aids if needed.
- **M**ap out your next day.
- **B**oycott blue light.
- **E**nter a blissful state with bedtime affirmations.
- **R**ead a book that makes you feel good.
- **S**leep like a baby.

While this may or may not feel like a lot at first glance, these steps are quite simple and will likely become automatic and effortless for you rather quickly. And while each of these steps can be extremely beneficial on its own, like the S.A.V.E.R.S., when combined, they can completely transform how you feel every night before bed and how well you sleep. Let's explore and expand on each step.

Stop Eating 3 to 4 Hours Before Bed

As mentioned in Chapter 8, digesting food is one of the most energy-depleting processes that our body endures (just think of how utterly exhausted you feel after eating a large meal). And while that might trick us into thinking that eating a meal before bed is a good strategy, since it makes us feel tired, the impact of eating close to bedtime is detrimental because it forces your body to continue working through the night and can leave you feeling like you were hit by a truck in the morning. So, being intentional about what time you eat, how much you eat, and which foods you eat is crucial to optimizing your sleep and how you feel in the morning.

Although it can take between 24 and 72 hours for a meal to move entirely through your GI (gastrointestinal) tract, what we're concerned with here are the three to four hours it takes for food to move from your stomach to your small intestine. That phase of the digestive process is where most of the heavy lifting occurs, and then your body can rest, heal, and rejuvenate while you're sleeping.

The length of time it takes for a meal to be digested is based on variables such as the quantity and types of food consumed. For example, foods that are high in fiber are much easier and faster to digest than foods that have a low fiber content. Two to three hours should be sufficient to digest high-fiber foods, such as most fruits, vegetables, nuts, beans, and whole grains. It might take four hours (or longer) to digest foods low in fiber, such as meat, bread, pasta, chips, and foods that are high in sugar. And, of course, the larger the meal, the longer it takes your body to digest.

I recommend working toward being able to finish your last meal of the day three to four hours before your bedtime. For example, if you go to bed at 10 PM, I recommend eating dinner around 6 or 6:30 PM to allow your body adequate time to digest. If your schedule or forces outside of your control leave you with no other option than to eat closer to bedtime, I suggest eating as small a meal as possible (smaller than the size of your fist) and choosing healthy foods, preferably those that are high in fiber.

If you are currently in the routine of eating dinner closer to bedtime or snacking late at night, understand that this will require a conscious effort and commitment on your part. To make it easier on yourself, I encourage you to *gradually* move up the time you finish your last meal so that your body and mind can acclimate. In other words, if you currently finish eating one hour before bedtime, try moving that up to finish 90 minutes before bedtime. Do that for a week, and then move to two hours, and then to two and a half, three, and so on. Include this change as part of your 30-Day Journey, and within a few weeks, this will start to become natural, automatic, and easy for you.

Your choice is to either eat close to bedtime, burden your body with the task of digesting food while it's supposed to be resting, and suffer the consequences in the morning—or start making a conscious decision to finish eating earlier and give your body an opportunity to rest, heal, and rejuvenate while you're sleeping so you wake up feeling reenergized.

Let Go of Stressful Thoughts and Feelings

Do you find that as you lay down to sleep, you are often consumed by thoughts about things that are out of your immediate control? As in, you ruminate over things that you can't (or won't) do anything about in the present moment?

Maybe your thoughts are directed toward something that happened in the recent past or your to-do list for the next day. Maybe you're worried about all your unfinished projects, your financial situation, health challenges, a conflict you're experiencing in a personal or professional relationship, a loved one who is suffering, the state of the world, the economy, or anything else that you have no control over as you lay down to go to sleep. The problem is that when we worry about things that are out of our immediate control, we naturally feel out of control, and that causes us to experience sleep-disrupting stress and anxiety.

Put another way, when we worry about things that are out of our control, we feel *unsafe*, and feeling safe is our most fundamental psychological need. When we don't feel safe, our nervous system engages our fight-or-flight response. It is nearly impossible to relax and fall asleep peacefully when we feel like our safety is threatened in some way. Thankfully, unless we are in some sort of immediate danger, feeling safe is a conscious choice that we can make. By simply acknowledging and affirming that we are indeed safe as we lay down to sleep, we can enter a state of psychological safety.

I used to spend most nights thinking and/or worrying about all the above until I had a breakthrough of what might seem to be an obvious realization: *my only objective at bedtime is to prepare my mind and body for blissful sleep.* That's it. Nothing else. Therefore, all our thoughts (or lack thereof) and actions should be in alignment with that singular objective.

Allow me to take a moment to clarify what I mean by "blissful" sleep. I define a state of bliss as feeling completely at peace and deeply grateful. This means that when my head hits the pillow, I am no longer going to ruminate over or replay what happened that day *unless* it is something that supports me feeling at peace and grateful. There's nothing wrong with thinking over your day as you fall asleep *if it brings a smile to your face.* But avoid allowing yourself to replay stressful events, think about what went wrong that day, or worry about the not-yet-here future, because those thought patterns can be detrimental to your ability to get restful and restorative sleep.

With this awareness, I decided that I needed to start flipping my mental "off" switch once it was time to wind down for the night. I needed to either stop thinking about things that caused me stress (easier said than done) or to replace those counterproductive thoughts with productive ones that supported me in feeling calm, peaceful, grateful, happy, or any other state that helped me to make the transition to blissful sleep. To do this, I implemented the following process of acknowledging, accepting, and then letting go of stressful thoughts and feelings in three effortless steps.

The first step in letting go of stressful feelings is to *acknowledge what you're feeling and the perceived cause*. Allowing yourself to dwell in a stressful emotional state and focus on anything that is out of your immediate control—right before bed—is not productive and robs you of feeling at peace as you prepare to fall asleep. However, attempting to ignore, suppress, or bypass a painful emotion is equally unproductive, as it doesn't address the feeling and usually perpetuates it underneath the surface.

To truly let go of a stressful feeling, you must bring it from your unconscious to your conscious mind so that you can acknowledge it, process it, and let it go. Here's an affirmation you can follow to do exactly that. Begin by taking a slow, deep breath as you identify and acknowledge what you're feeling and what's causing it.

I am feeling _____ [fear, anxiety, anger, stress, sadness, frustration, or any other sleep-disrupting emotion] about _____ [insert the perceived cause of your inner turmoil].

Here are some examples:

- I am feeling fear about my financial situation.
- I am feeling angry about how my spouse treated me today.
- I am feeling sadness about my health challenges.

As you begin to acknowledge and name what you're feeling, take slow deep breaths to calm your mind and your nervous system. And be patient, as it may take a minute or so to become present to your true feelings. Acknowledge whatever emotions you're experiencing from a place of acceptance and nonjudgment. There's no need to label your feelings or yourself as good or bad. Simply observe what you're feeling and where it's coming from as you relax into each breath.

The second step is to *remember your primary bedtime objective—preparing your mind and body for blissful sleep—and give yourself permission to completely accept and be at peace with whatever you're feeling.* Even if what you're feeling is unpleasant, resisting the feeling only amplifies your inner turmoil because resisting reality perpetuates emotional pain and is a form of making yourself wrong for feeling the way you do. When we resist the way we're feeling, we not only feel bad but also feel bad that we feel bad. Instead, remind yourself that you have every right to feel the way you do, but that right now—bedtime—is simply not the time to indulge those feelings and perpetuate unnecessary stress. Try this affirmation:

> Though I have every right to feel the way I do, now is not the time to dwell on a stressful state. My only objective is to prepare my mind and body for blissful sleep, so I will align my thoughts and feelings with that objective.

Give yourself grace, be at peace with whatever you're feeling, and remember that now is the time to align your thoughts and feelings with your primary bedtime objective: to prepare your mind and body for an optimal night of sleep.

The third and final step is to *give yourself permission to let go of stressful thoughts and fall asleep feeling good.* Only you can give yourself permission to let go of your stressful thoughts and feel good and grateful as you drift off to sleep. Try this affirmation:

> I give myself permission to let go of any stressful thoughts and feelings, and instead, I am choosing

to be at peace and focus on what I'm grateful for
so that I can feel blissful as I drift off to sleep.

If giving yourself permission to let go of your stressful thoughts and to fall asleep feeling good is a permission you haven't granted yourself in a while, it may feel foreign at first. If the idea of feeling blissful as you drift off to sleep sounds impossible, understand that it's likely just because you haven't been doing it. But you absolutely can. Remember, it's not about what's happening outside of you but inside of you that determines how you feel. Stick with it until it becomes your norm.

Use Natural Sleep Aids If Needed

In case you struggle to fall asleep or stay asleep, I would be remiss if I didn't share the sleep supplements that I used to help me overcome the agonizing six-month period when I suffered from chronic insomnia and sleep deprivation.

I went on a search for natural remedies and solutions. I began experimenting with a wide variety of sleep supplements, being mindful of every ingredient and looking for those that didn't contain synthetic fillers and that were plant-based and organic whenever possible. I eventually called Dr. Michael Breus and asked for his expert advice. Michael was a clinical psychologist and sleep medicine expert, known as the Sleep Doctor. He responded by asking me a lot of questions about my diet, medications, and supplements, then he made his recommendations. I immediately put everything I had learned into practice.

Within a matter of weeks, I went from averaging an unbearable two to four hours of sleep per night to a much healthier six to seven hours and woke up feeling great. After searching for and trying different sleep supplements, here's the regimen I landed on that finally worked:

90 minutes before bed . . .

- 450mg organic valerian root (brand I use: Herbal Roots, available at Amazon.com)
- 300mg magnesium glycinate (brand I use: Organifi. Note: Organifi is one of my podcast sponsors, so you can get 20 percent off at organifi.com/tmm)

45 minutes before bed . . .

- CBN Night Caps (brand I use: Cured Nutrition, who is also one of my podcast sponsors, so you can get 20 percent off at www.curednutrition.com/tmm.)

30 minutes before bed . . .

- 3mg melatonin (brand I use: Herbatonin, available at Amazon.com)

Since I began applying this supplement regimen as part of my Miracle Evening more than two years ago, I have averaged seven hours of quality sleep each night. I have also gifted these supplements to friends who were struggling with sleep, and the results have been promising for nearly every person I've gifted them to. However, because every *body* is unique, even natural herbs and supplements can be unsafe for someone with certain medical conditions or cause unwanted side effects. I discovered that I was allergic to ashwagandha after I had been taking it for a few months, and it was contributing to the anxiety and sleeplessness I was experiencing. So, you should always consult a trusted medical professional before taking any supplements.

Also, to be clear, sleep supplements alone didn't cure my insomnia. They were simply one component of my approach. If I had continued to eat too close to bedtime, or allowed myself to think stressful thoughts as I lay down to sleep, I don't think the supplements would have made much of an impact.

Sleep aids may not be necessary for you, but if they are, you may find these natural supplements to be life savers.

Map Out Your Next Day

Before bed, make sure everything is out of your head that you need to do tomorrow. Whether that means you use a digital calendar or you physically write down your tasks in a journal or a planner that you keep on your bedside table, map out your schedule hour by hour (including free time). An alternative to doing this at bedtime is to do this at the end of your workday so that you don't even have to think about it before bed. Either way, writing down what you need to do the next day helps clear your mind and reduce stress. Gino Wickman talks about this in *Entrepreneurial Leap*:

> Every night before I go to bed, I lay out my entire next day on a legal pad. I use a legal pad because I believe in the power of writing by hand. I time-block everything I need to do: the calls I need to make, the meetings I need to attend, and the projects I need to finish. I list them all in chronological order so that my day is already charted.
>
> If you do this, you will sleep better. You will wake up with ideas and be more creative. You'll wake up with answers to problems and projects you need to work on the next day. That's because your subconscious will be working on them during the night while you sleep.

Personally, I use a digital calendar, an app called Fantastical, which is similar to Google Calendar, for my schedule. I prefer a digital calendar because most of my activities each day are recurring, such as *Miracle Morning / S.A.V.E.R.S.* (4 to 5 AM), *Writing* (5 to 6 AM), *Top Work Priority* (6 to 7 AM), *Family Time + Smoothie* (7 to 8 AM), *Workout + Prep for My Workday* (8 to 9 AM), *Emails* (9 to 10 AM), and so on. They are already time blocked, and I rarely have to give my schedule any thought as I lay down to go to sleep. By putting your schedule in writing, whether on paper or digitally, you can rest assured that you have budgeted time to tackle all your important tasks the next day. When the next day's responsibilities are in writing, you no longer have to give them any thought and can focus on your objective of sleeping peacefully.

Boycott Blue Light Before Bed

If you have trouble falling asleep at night, your use of electronics might be to blame. Cell phones, tablets, computers, and televisions all emit blue light. Also known as high-energy visible (HEV) light, blue light produces higher amounts of energy and boosts attention and alertness. It also limits your body's production of melatonin, the hormone that makes you sleepy. So, if you have a habit of looking at your smartphone or watching TV too close to bedtime, it is likely disrupting the quality of your sleep.

How can we eliminate or at least minimize blue light exposure before bed? Here are a few tips:

- **Avoid looking at electronics 30 to 60 minutes before bed.** While avoiding blue light two to three hours before bed is ideal, start with 30 to 60 minutes. To help you do this, you might choose to set a reminder in your phone that prompts you to stop looking at your phone (I know, the irony).
- **Keep your bedroom as dark as possible.** Dim your lights 30 minutes before bed. You can also use red light bulbs since red light waves are less likely to affect circadian

rhythms and suppress melatonin. I use a red bulb in my bedside lamp.

- **Plug your phone in across the room.** We addressed this tip earlier as part of the five-step snooze-proof wake-up strategy, but I think it's important to revisit it here. In addition to emitting blue light, the content on your phone is also stimulating and can make you more alert at the time when you want to be winding down. If you have trouble resisting the temptation of your phone as you try to fall asleep, plug it in across the room or even in the bathroom. This way, you cannot absentmindedly reach for it while you're going to sleep. And remember that keeping your alarm out of reach ensures that you have to get out of bed to turn it off in the morning, which makes it easier to stay awake.

Enter a Blissful State with Bedtime Affirmations

Letting go of stressful thoughts and emotions can be much easier when you have peaceful, calming, and empowering thoughts and emotions to replace them with. To foster peaceful thinking, I use the following bedtime affirmations, which I think to myself as I breathe deeply and slowly and drift off to sleep. I invite you to take a few moments to pause after you read each one, take a deep breath, possibly close your eyes, and do your best to really feel what you're affirming.

To accept whatever happened that day, release any resistance, and be completely at peace, try this affirmation:

Now is not the time to worry about or try and solve my problems. My only objective is to calm my mind and body for restful and rejuvenating sleep.

To be completely present to the perfection of the moment, try this affirmation:

This moment is perfect. I am safe, and I am comfortable in my bed. I have nothing to worry about.

To express, experience, and embody gratitude, try this affirmation:

I am grateful for _____. OR
God, thank you for _____.

If you currently have a habit of thinking stressful thoughts before bed, recognize that it will take a conscious commitment to replace them with peaceful, grateful thoughts. Our programmed way of thinking is habitual and mostly unconscious, so your subconscious may resist new thoughts and want to default to old ones (that's normal and expected). Having written affirmations can be one of the simplest and most effective ways to take control of your thoughts and choose those that best serve you.

The following is a more detailed version of my personal bedtime affirmations that I created long before I ever thought of writing this book. I printed them out, kept them on my bedside table, and read them every night right before I lay down to go to sleep. Doing so helped remind me of my primary intention of relaxing my mind and body to prepare for blissful sleep. Of course, these, too, have been expanded and updated for this book.

Miracle Evening Bedtime Affirmations

I commit to reading my bedtime affirmations every night, before bed, to prepare my mind and body for blissful sleep and set an empowering intention to wake up feeling energized and excited!

First: I have completed all the tasks necessary to prepare myself for tomorrow, including setting out everything that I need for my Miracle Morning (book, journal, workout clothes, water, etc.). I've also moved my alarm clock across the room so that I will need get out of bed to turn it off, since it's much easier to stay awake once I'm already out of bed and moving my body.

Second: I'm going to bed at _____ PM and waking up at _____ AM, which will give me roughly ___ hours of sleep. This is plenty because I know that how I feel when I wake up is influenced by the intention I set now. So, regardless of how long it takes me to fall asleep, I will wake up feeling energized, excited, and inspired to create the most extraordinary life I can imagine— because I and the people I love deserve nothing less!

Third: I am committed to waking up on time tomorrow for my Miracle Morning because, by doing so, I am becoming the person I need to be to create everything I want for my life. I'm anticipating the morning with positive expectations and excitement (!) because I am fully aware of the benefits that I'll receive by starting my day with my S.A.V.E.R.S., so I will jump out of bed with energy and enthusiasm!

Fourth: My only objective right now is to prepare my mind and body for blissful sleep. So, I give myself permission to let go of *all* stressful thoughts. Now is not the time to worry about or try and solve my problems. This moment is perfect. I am safe. I am comfortable in my bed. I have nothing to worry about. If I think of anything, I will direct my focus toward something I'm grateful for and feel a calming sense of gratitude so that I can dwell in a peaceful mental and emotional state that fosters blissful sleep.

I often see Miracle Morning Community members post about how helpful these bedtime affirmations have been to their ability to wake up effectively each morning. One member of the Miracle Morning Community said that he read them every night before bed for 48 consecutive days and never missed a single Miracle Morning. Then, the first night he failed to read his bedtime affirmations, he slept through his alarm the next day.

If you'd prefer to print a copy of these affirmations to keep next to your bed, so it's easier for you to remember to actually read them each night, you can download them at MiracleMorning .com/resources.

Read a Book That Makes You Feel Good

As I said earlier, reading is the most immediate, surefire way to acquire knowledge and set the tone for your day, or in this case, night. I also mentioned the importance of thinking positive thoughts before you go to bed. Well, guess what? Reading can help us with this. Pick up a novel that always brings a smile to your face, a book about being happy, or anything that makes you feel good and calms your mind.

Personally, I get into bed, put my phone on airplane mode, turn on my white noise machine, and pull out a book from a rotating collection that I keep in the drawer of my nightstand. Reading for 10 to 20 minutes before bed helps me get into a positive state of mind before I close my eyes. To do this, there are two very specific criteria for what I read:

- It must be a book that makes me feel good, grateful, and/or peaceful so that it contributes to preparing my mind for blissful sleep.
- It's almost always a book I've already read and in which I've underlined the parts I want to reread, so I don't exert any energy trying to comprehend or learn something new.

Although it's not necessary to choose books that you've already read, this approach requires far less mental bandwidth. This is very different than the books I read during my Miracle Morning, when I usually select something *new* that teaches me how to improve or achieve a specific result in a particular area of my life, which takes a lot of mental bandwidth.

After reading, I am primed to begin thinking about what I am grateful for, to meditate, or to recite a mantra as I drift off to sleep.

Sleep Like a Baby

This last step is as much philosophical and spiritual as it is practical. Consider that when you came into this world, you were born into a pure, unaffected state of consciousness, with no worries, regrets, opinions, judgments, expectations, insecurities, fears, or belief systems thrust upon you by other people that told you how you were supposed to think, feel, and behave. You weren't afraid of failure, stressed about problems, or concerned with what other people thought of you. Your mind wasn't yet programmed with society's invented norms, standards, and rules. You had no negative judgments of others nor any about yourself. And you certainly didn't lay awake at night ruminating over the past or worrying about the future.

Without any effort, joy was your default state of being, which was disturbed only by occasional physical discomforts, such as hunger pains or lack of sleep. As soon as you were fed or took a nap, you were back to smiling, giggling, and observing. There's a reason babies are often referred to as "bundles of joy." Joy is our natural, inherent state.

But as you got older, everything changed. Your natural states of Inner Freedom and inherent joy were gradually eroded by external programming. Growing up, we are conditioned by our parents and society at large to think that joy and happiness are found in things outside of ourselves. A cartoon. A toy. Food. Praise. Accomplishments. However, none of those things actually provide us with true, sustained joy and happiness. These external stimuli produce short-lived emotional highs and states of pleasure that quickly dissipate and must be replaced by another stimulus.

It is time to get back to your inherent state of Inner Freedom, and bedtime is the perfect opportunity to start, by taking control of your mental and emotional well-being. You don't have to lay awake at night ruminating over the past or worrying about the future. Of course, you can if you want, but that's up to you.

Remember, the realization (and resulting decision) that took me from chronic insomnia, sleep deprivation, severe anxiety, and depression to sleeping like a baby was this: *My only objective at bedtime is to prepare my mind and body for blissful sleep.* That's it. Nothing else.

What does this look like in practice? I implement every single step outlined in the S.L.U.M.B.E.R.S. And as I lay down to go to sleep, I spend a few minutes thinking of what I'm grateful for and allowing myself to dwell on a feeling of gratitude. Personally, I find it helpful to direct that gratitude toward God, thinking something like, *God, thank you so much for my wife, Ursula. I am so blessed to have her in my life*. Then I will breathe slowly and deeply as I think of Ursula and give myself the gift of dwelling on an all-encompassing state of gratitude. I'll then move on to other aspects of my life that I'm grateful for, such as my children, my health, our home, my comfortable bed, and so on.

Other times, if I had a good day overall, I'll replay the events of the day, such as thanking God and feeling grateful that I got to play a board game with my son, for the meaningful conversation I had with my daughter, the progress I made at work, and the meal that my wife made for our family.

Typically, this routine lulls me to sleep. But for the times that it doesn't, I will continue focusing on my breathing and what I'm grateful for while reciting calming affirmations until I finally drift off to sleep, feeling grateful and at peace.

By focusing on what you are grateful for, you can enter a peaceful state of contentment before bedtime and give your subconscious the gift of a nighttime's worth of happy thoughts. It was not necessarily easy to practice these methods at the start, and you should not expect it to be. If you're not used to consciously focusing on and feeling what you're grateful for, this might seem foreign or unrealistic at first. Again, our thought patterns are mostly unconscious and habitual, so it takes a conscious effort and time to upgrade our thinking. Reciting bedtime affirmations that remind you of what to focus on definitely helps. Over time, it became increasingly easier for me to think positive thoughts before bed and to prepare myself for restful sleep, until it was unconscious and automatic. Before I knew it, I went from lying awake feeling stressed every night to falling asleep feeling genuinely grateful and at peace. And not only did I fall asleep that way, but I woke up feeling the same!

Sleep is one of the most beneficial gifts we give to our minds and bodies, and with S.L.U.M.B.E.R.S., you are perfectly prepared to make the most of that gift.

Customizing Your Own Miracle Evening

Just like the S.A.V.E.R.S., your Miracle Evening routine can be adjusted, customized, and tailored to fit your schedule and preferences. Just as this book is about establishing *your* Miracle Morning ritual, this chapter is about designing *your* Miracle Evening ritual. You can implement every step outlined in the S.L.U.M.B.E.R.S., pick and choose which steps resonate with you, or start from scratch and build your own ritual. What is important is not which version you choose but that you implement some type of evening ritual that helps you relax your mind and body so that you can get a good night's sleep and wake up feeling rested and rejuvenated.

There is certainly something to be said for keeping it simple. For example, you might simply choose to stop eating a few hours before bed and think about what you're grateful for as you fall asleep, and that is all you need to wind down and sleep well. To help you do that, here are the essential outcomes to keep in mind when deciding on your Miracle Evening routine:

- Let go of stressful thoughts and feelings so you can go to bed feeling calm and relaxed.
- Set up your internal and external environments to wake up feeling more refreshed and energized.
- Drift off to sleep feeling grateful and at peace.

Some other strategies to consider are using eye masks and ear-plugs to help eliminate the possibility of your sleep being disrupted by light or sound. The use of white or brown noise can also be help-ful for some sleepers. Personally, I use both earplugs and a "white noise" app that runs from across the room while my phone is in air-plane mode. This helps to drown out any unexpected noises that could disrupt your sleep.

Final Thoughts on the Miracle Evening

You now have the building blocks to create your ideal Miracle Evening ritual that will complement your Miracle Morning. Remember that maintaining a new routine requires a commitment at first but can start to become automatic and effortless quickly (usually within a few weeks). So, have faith in the process and remember that the benefits you'll experience are significant, and it will become easier and easier every time that you do it.

Remember that how you end your day may be as important as how you begin it. While your Miracle Morning enables you to start each day in a peak mental, emotional, physical, and spiritual state, your Miracle Evening routine allows you to end each day feeling grateful and at peace so that you can drift off into blissful sleep and wake up feeling good.

I can tell you from experience that, no matter how much you might struggle right now with letting go of stressful thoughts and getting a good night's sleep, implementing a Miracle Evening ritual can be as transformative for you as it was for me. You deserve to fall asleep feeling at peace and grateful, and only you can give that gift to yourself. Follow the S.L.U.M.B.E.R.S. tonight, and may you wake up feeling rested, rejuvenated, and ready for your Miracle Morning so you can show up at your best—for those you love, those you lead, and for yourself—every single day.

12

THE MIRACLE LIFE

Your Path to Inner Freedom

"If you want to, you can find a million reasons to hate life and be angry at the world. Or, if you want to, you could find a million reasons to love life and be happy. Choose wisely."
—Cari Welsh

"What you'll find is that the only thing you really want from life is to feel enthusiasm, joy, and love. If you can feel that all the time, who cares what happens outside? If you can always feel up, if you can always feel excited about the experience of the moment, then it doesn't make any difference what the experience is."
—Michael Singer

I magine, for a moment, that I was to magically appear in front of you, right now, as a genie. Picture it: I'm floating in front of you, legs crossed, levitating in midair (stick with me, I know this just got weird), and I tell you that I can grant you one wish, but it is a very specific type of wish.

I can't give you a fancy mansion or a pile of money. I can't make you younger or change your physical appearance. I can't make any person in your life more enjoyable to be around (sorry, I know that one would probably be super helpful), and I definitely can't grant you a thousand more wishes.

The one and only wish I have the power to grant for you is to give you the limitless ability to choose how you experience every moment of your life, regardless of how difficult your circumstances or the people around you may be. In other words, you could choose your optimal mental and emotional state in every moment—to live unconsumed by fear, stress, and worry, to wake up every day and truly love your life, live in a state of bliss, be the happiest you've ever been, experience heaven on earth, you name it—every day, for the rest of your life. What would you wish for? How would you choose to experience every moment of your life?

The problem is that we've been conditioned to believe that our mental and emotional well-being are dictated by outside forces. We mistakenly believe that *when good things happen, I feel good, and when bad things happen, I feel bad*. So, we allow circumstances, events, and other people to determine how we feel and, ultimately, our experience of life. The Miracle Life offers us a new, far more empowering paradigm: *no matter what happens, I feel however I choose to feel*.

The solution is learning how to take control of your mental and emotional state so that you can proactively choose how you experience each moment of your life—a concept you've already been introduced to earlier in the book with Emotional Optimization Meditation.

The Miracle Life is a concept that evolved out of over a decade of practicing the Miracle Morning with a focus on elevating my own consciousness. To understand the fundamental difference between these two and how they complement one another, consider that the Miracle Morning is a practice for personal development, while the Miracle Life is a paradigm for personal fulfillment. The Miracle Morning enables you to develop the mindset, habits, and capabilities you need to create the circumstances you want for your life, and the Miracle Life unlocks your ability to experience optimal states of consciousness so that you can be genuinely happy and enjoy the life you have—no matter what your circumstances are.

The Miracle Life is your path to Inner Freedom, and Inner Freedom is the fundamental state of consciousness from which you are free to choose how you interpret and experience each moment. This state of consciousness is inherently available to every single one of us regardless of our circumstances. We gain access to this state of consciousness when we stop mistakenly believing that outside forces are responsible for why we feel the way we do, learn how to be at peace with things we can't change, and no longer allow ourselves to get upset over the aspects of life that are out of our control.

Imagine being able to consciously choose your ideal mental and emotional state in each moment, to be completely at peace and undisturbed no matter what you're facing in life. Imagine discovering that you have a superpower that enables you to decide how you want to feel, to be genuinely at peace and as happy as you've ever been, even during the most difficult circumstances you've ever faced. This is what the Miracle Life enables you to do.

In other words, the Miracle Life isn't a change in your circumstances; it is a complete transformation of *how you experience your circumstances*. It is a process of elevating and then conditioning your consciousness to a state of Inner Freedom so that you are completely free to choose what you think and how you feel in each moment. As the quote from Cari Welsh that opened this chapter so clearly stated, "If you want to, you can find a million reasons to hate life and be angry at the world. Or, if you want to, you could find a million reasons to love life and be happy. Choose wisely."

The Primary Obstacle to Inner Freedom: Inner Turmoil

Consider that two different people can have nearly identical circumstances or endure similar tragedies, and one person is miserable—constantly suffering and complaining about how bad their life is—while the other person is completely at peace, genuinely happy, and consistently expresses and experiences gratitude for how blessed they are to be alive. How is that possible? Despite having the same circumstances, two radically different paradigms create two radically different ways of experiencing life. Which would you choose? Are you aware that you have a choice?

When choosing between these two paradigms, most if not all of us would surely choose to be the person who is completely at peace, genuinely happy, and consistently experiencing and expressing gratitude for how blessed *we* are to be alive. We all want happier, more peaceful, and more fulfilled lives. Unfortunately, most of us don't allow ourselves to be happy and experience sustained feelings of peace and fulfillment because we've unconsciously agreed that outside forces—other people, events, circumstances, and our past—have the power to determine how we feel.

As a result, most of us go through life enduring suboptimal mental and emotional states such as stress, fear, anxiety, anger, guilt, shame, resentment, hate, and other forms of emotional pain—and we miss out on states of peace, love, joy, gratitude, confidence, happiness, and even bliss, which are always available to us.

We continue to suffer because no one taught us how to harness our inherent ability to consciously choose how we experience each moment. This is especially true during times of adversity when life is difficult or painful, or when we're facing challenges that may seem insurmountable and feeling hopeless.

To elevate our consciousness to a state of Inner Freedom, we must identify and transcend any underlying obstacle that is preventing us from doing so. And while we could certainly come up with an endless list of *external* obstacles for why we're stressed out or unhappy (our financial situation, our past trauma, the actions of other people, or any difficult circumstances that we blame for the way we feel inside), we can narrow all of them down to one, single, fundamental, underlying *internal* obstacle that prevents us from living in a state of Inner Freedom.

What is this underlying obstacle? Inner turmoil.

We experience inner turmoil in the form of suboptimal mental and emotional states, such as fear, shame, guilt, regret, anger, or helplessness. Although Inner Freedom is the state that we were born into and is always available to us, inner turmoil prevents us from experiencing love, joy, peace, happiness, clarity, confidence, and other positive mental and emotional states that we desire. When you endure any degree of inner turmoil, you block yourself from experiencing your inherent, liberating state of Inner Freedom. You cannot experience both simultaneously, so you are always choosing between the two.

Choosing to experience life in a state of Inner Freedom requires that we transcend the obstacle of inner turmoil. To transcend any obstacle, we must identify the causes so that we can overcome them. If we're not clear on what's causing us to endure suboptimal mental and emotional states, we won't be able to address the root cause and overcome it.

The Causes of Inner Turmoil

There is both an overarching and an underlying cause of inner turmoil. The overarching cause is our allowing outside forces to determine our mental and emotional well-being. We naturally (and mistakenly) think the things we're upset about are what's causing us to be upset. On the surface, that seems completely logical, but it's not the case.

When we face any degree of adversity, whether a minor annoyance or a major tragedy, we naturally resist reality and wish things were different. What we are unaware of is that our *resistance to reality* is the cause of our emotional pain—not the thing we're upset about. And the degree to which we resist reality and wish things that we have no control over were different determines the degree of emotional pain that we create for ourselves.

The underlying cause of all inner turmoil and emotional pain is our unconscious resistance to reality—wishing things that are out of our control were different.

What's worse is that resisting our reality doesn't change things; it only causes us to create and perpetuate unnecessary feelings of stress, fear, anger, resentment, and any other form of emotional pain that perpetuate suffering and rob us of our freedom to be at peace and enjoy life.

Your Path to Inner Freedom

The Miracle Life is based on a timeless concept but one that escapes most people: we were born with the inherent freedom to choose how we experience each moment. This ability is harnessed by actively elevating and conditioning our state of consciousness to that of *Inner Freedom*.

Inner freedom is not a new concept and has been a primary aim of not only sages and philosophers but also anyone who has aspired to experience life in a truly liberated state. In 1941, Paramahansa Yogananda, author of the spiritual classic *Autobiography of a Yogi*, wrote that "inner freedom is the ability to do all things guided by wisdom." Deepak Chopra advocates that "the most precious freedom is inner freedom." In the 21st century, millions have been introduced to the concept of Inner Freedom through Michael Singer's books *The Untethered Soul* and *Living Untethered*, in which he states, "Only you can take inner freedom away from yourself or give it to yourself. Nobody else can. It doesn't matter what others do unless you decide that it matters to you."

While emotions are short-lived and fleeting, states of consciousness are our underlying way of experiencing life. Inner Freedom is a fundamental state of consciousness that is based on being completely at peace with all aspects of life so that nothing external has the power to determine your mental or emotional states. When that is the case, you get to choose how you experience any given moment that you are alive.

Most people have very little awareness that Inner Freedom is available to them. Their inner state is at the mercy of their external circumstances. If they wake up late for work, get into a fight with their spouse, or receive an angry email from a customer, they allow it to affect how they feel even to the point of *letting it* ruin their entire day. If they miss a flight, they are upset and stew over it for hours.

While most of us may have never realized that we have unlimited access to our inherent Inner Freedom and continue to suffer from varying degrees of inner turmoil, emotional pain, and instability, there are countless examples of people throughout history who have shown us that this liberating state is available to *all* of us, no matter how difficult our circumstances may be.

Consider famed psychiatrist and author Viktor Frankl. In his book *Man's Search for Meaning*, Frankl describes that in 1942, he and his family were sent to the Theresienstadt concentration camp, where his father died. Then in 1944, he and the members of his family who were still alive were taken to Auschwitz, where his mother and brother were murdered. His wife would die in yet another concentration camp. He endured all this while under the harsh conditions of starvation, sleep deprivation, and psychological torture.

We can all agree that what Frankl experienced was horrifying to a degree beyond what most of us have ever experienced. And yet, drawing on his studies as a psychologist, he was able to find meaning in his life regardless of his circumstances. How did he do this? By realizing that though his external freedom was being restricted by other people, he could focus on his inherent Inner Freedom to choose his experience of life amid death and destruction.

In Frankl's words, "Everything can be taken from a man but one thing: the last of human freedoms—to choose one's attitude in any given set of circumstances."

In other words, Inner Freedom is realized not by changing your circumstances but by elevating your consciousness so that you are free to choose how you experience your circumstances. No matter how difficult your life has been, is now, or may be in the future, you always have the freedom to choose how you experience each moment.

Could it be that human beings were born with the freedom to be genuinely happy and enjoy this one life we've been given? Is it possible that there is nothing to pursue and that life itself contains an unlimited supply of true, sustainable joy, but our collective problem is that we unconsciously adhere to society's paradigms that block us from experiencing all that life has to offer?

Happiness Is a Choice

When I was 19 years old, my mentor Jesse Levine taught me a way of taking total responsibility for my happiness and never blaming my emotional state on anyone or anything else. Although I didn't fully comprehend the impact that lesson would make in my life, it would ultimately transform my ability to choose how I experienced every moment that was to come. This would become particularly invaluable in preparing me to face the unimaginable adversities that lay ahead.

Jesse taught me that "happiness is a choice—it's up to us to choose whether or not we're happy." I don't know how you react to that statement, but when I first heard this, I wasn't buying it. My paradigm was, "When things in life are going well, I feel happy. When things aren't going well, I don't feel happy." Pretty standard.

Then, he explained that in life, there are essentially two metaphorical pages that we can choose to focus on at any given moment. One page lists everything that we have to feel bad about (our problems, fears, regrets, physical pain, past traumas, people we don't like, etc.—the list is endless), and the other page lists everything that we have to feel good about, much of which we often take for granted (our health, our life, the present moment, the roof over our head, the people we love, the food we have to eat, our connection with God, nature, etc.—this list is also endless).

Every human being on planet Earth—from those who are suffering unimaginable pain or tragedy to those we assume have it easier or better than we do—has access to both pages. The key is understanding that which page we consciously *choose* to give our attention to is arguably the most significant influence on how we feel at any given moment.

This is why there are people who are considered to be "highly successful" in modern society (e.g., millionaires, celebrities, etc.), and who seem to have everything they've ever wanted, who are noticeably miserable, while some villagers in developing countries who live below the poverty line (but are deeply grateful for everything they have) smile from ear to ear at the difficult life they're blessed to live.

You may know someone who constantly complains about their life and then justifies their complaining by saying something like, "I'm not being negative; I'm just being realistic."

Really? Let's ask ourselves how it is any more realistic to dwell on and complain about the aspects of ourselves and our lives that make us feel bad than it is to dwell on and celebrate the good in our lives? Both perspectives are *equally* realistic, but which page we choose to focus on (most of the time) determines how we feel (most of the time).

So, maybe Jesse was right. Maybe happiness *is* a choice, and we do get to choose whether we're happy based on which page of life we choose to focus on, more often than not.

When I woke up from a coma at age 20, after barely surviving a head-on car crash with a drunk driver, I made the conscious decision that I would strive to be the happiest and most grateful I had ever been *while* I endured the most difficult time in my life. Thanks to the empowering paradigm that Jesse had taught me just 18 months prior, I was able to do exactly that. By accepting my circumstances exactly as they were, being at peace with all that I couldn't change, and focusing my energy and attention on the page in my life that listed everything I had to be grateful for (while proactively doing everything in my power to create the outcomes I wanted), I was able to enjoy each moment amid my seemingly insurmountable adversity.

I know from experience that life can be both chronically and unexpectedly difficult. I also believe we may look back one day and regret all the time we spent blaming our outside forces for how we feel and not allowing ourselves to be happy. You already have everything you need to be the happiest you could ever be. It's called *life*. Either you enjoy it, or you don't. But we must understand that blaming our inner turmoil on external forces is robbing all of us of being happy and enjoying our lives.

Let's explore how you can use three simple steps to accept the aspects of life that are out of your control, allow yourself to be at peace with what you can't change, be the most grateful you have ever been, and give yourself permission to be happy and enjoy this one life you've been blessed to live.

The ABCs of the Miracle Life

Like the S.A.V.E.R.S. for the Miracle Morning, the Miracle Life can be remembered and implemented using a simple, memorable ABC formula. This is intentional. Mnemonic devices (like S.A.V.E.R.S.) have proven to be a highly effective technique for improving our memory retention and our ability to recall and implement information. The easier something is to remember, the more likely we are to retain it, which naturally increases the probability that we will continue to implement it.

Although the following formula is simple, like anything worthwhile it takes consistent practice to elevate and condition your consciousness so that it becomes automatic and nearly effortless. I recommend integrating these steps into your daily Miracle Morning practice so that the Miracle Life paradigm becomes deeply rooted in your subconscious. We'll address how to do that in the coming pages.

The good news is that most people find an immediate transformation in their awareness of how they experience each moment. Within a few weeks, or even days, it can dramatically impact your happiness and ability to remain at peace during situations that may have previously been a source of emotional pain and instability. Practicing it daily on the minor things (e.g., being stuck in traffic or a conflict with another person) builds your skills for the big things (e.g., enduring financial hardship, health challenges, loss of a loved one, or the breakup of a relationship).

A: Accept life exactly as it is. In life, things happen that we don't like. We encounter bumper-to-bumper traffic when we're running late. Our child struggles at school. Our spouse does things that drive us crazy. Our customer cancels an order. We get fired from our job. We get diagnosed with a serious illness. Someone we love passes away unexpectedly. It's human nature to get upset and reject these realities, wishing so badly that they were different. But our rejection of reality doesn't change anything. It just causes us to suffer and prevents us from being able to react constructively to the issue at hand. Once we understand that the cause of our emotional pain is our resistance to reality, we can see that the solution is learning how to accept life exactly as it is and allow ourselves to be at peace with reality.

B: Be grateful for each moment. Gratitude is a universal lens through which we can interpret and experience quite literally *any* moment of our lives, including the most difficult, unpleasant, and painful ones. While it's easy, natural, and extremely beneficial to feel grateful for the aspects of our life that are favorable, it can be even more beneficial to learn how to be genuinely grateful when faced with adversity. While being grateful for our adversity may seem counterintuitive, consider that every adversity provides us with an opportunity to learn, grow, and become better versions of who we were when we first encountered the difficulty. It is often the most difficult or painful times in our life that gift us with the greatest opportunities to evolve.

C: Choose your optimal state of consciousness. Remember that while emotions are often short-lived and fleeting, states of consciousness are underlying and ongoing ways of experiencing every moment of your life. In the moment that someone cuts you off in traffic, you may not have control over that flash of anger you have, but you can control how you feel next by choosing what you will focus on and which state of consciousness you will dwell on. You can decide the state to embody next is empathy. Perhaps that person was racing to the hospital to see their injured child. Perhaps they were just fired from their job. Or perhaps they simply didn't see you and made a mistake. Whatever the reasons, you can't change what happened. You can only choose how you experience each moment.

Let's dive deeper into understanding the nuances and benefits of each step.

Step A: Accept Life Exactly as It Is

Whether we face an unexpected challenge or chronic adversity and find ourselves feeling upset and wishing reality were different, we essentially have two fundamental choices:

- We can continue to unconsciously resist reality, wishing things that are out of our control were different and causing ourselves to experience ongoing inner turmoil, emotional pain, and instability.
- We can consciously choose to accept life exactly as it is, be at peace with what we can't change, focus on changing what we can, and identify our optimal mental and emotional states so that we can choose how we experience each moment of our lives.

When I began a career in direct sales at ninteen years old, another lesson I learned from my mentor was that the profession of selling is a microcosm for life, only with amplified adversity. In other words, he explained that, as a salesperson, I would experience challenges nearly every day (failure, rejection, disappointment, etc.) that most people only experience occasionally.

To effectively manage my mental and emotional states amid such challenges, he taught me another powerful strategy that I use to this day: the 5 Minute Rule. The rule states that when something happens that we don't like—whether a minor inconvenience or a major tragedy—it's okay to get upset for a short period, but there is no value in dwelling on something long after it happened, wishing it didn't happen, and feeling bad about it for an extended period of time.

He taught me to literally set a timer for five minutes, during which time I was allowed to bitch, moan, complain, cry, vent, feel sorry for myself, or indulge in whatever emotional response came up. Then, when the five-minute timer went off, he taught me to consciously accept whatever happened (or didn't happen) and move on. He also taught me to say three very impactful words when the timer went off, "Can't change it," as a reminder that there was no point in continuing to resist reality and wish the past were different. He explained that the only logical choice was to accept life exactly as it was and immediately focus 100 percent of my energy and attention on what was in my control.

When I first learned the 5 Minute Rule, I scoffed at it and thought, "Yeah right, I'm not going to get over something in five minutes just because I set a timer." But I also committed to sincerely trying it. After all, what did I have to lose?

A few days later, I experienced my first no-show. I had scheduled a Cutco presentation with a woman and drove 45 minutes to her house, but when I got there, no one was home. A note on the door read, "Sorry, we don't want any knives!" I couldn't believe it. Rather than at least giving me the courtesy of calling to cancel our appointment, she had allowed me to waste my time and drive all the way out to her house to find a note.

I went back to my car, grabbed my cell phone, and set a timer for five minutes. As I drove away, I started stewing over how disrespectful it was to let me drive that far and then miss our appointment. I thought about the income I lost out on by wasting my time when I could have been at another appointment. I worried about not reaching my goals. I considered whom I could complain to about this and rehearsed what I would say to make the story sound as dramatic as possible. Maybe you can relate?

Suddenly, I was startled when the alarm on my phone went off. I turned it off and said out loud to no one, "I'm still pissed off!" At least I felt justified in my assessment that five minutes wasn't enough time to get over being upset.

For the next few weeks, I continued applying the 5 Minute Rule. Surprisingly, it started making a major impact. After the five-minute timer would go off, I would take a deep breath and say, "Can't change it," a simple but powerful reminder that because I can't change what happened in the past—whether it was five minutes, five days, or five decades ago—the only productive choice I had was to accept life exactly as it was and take action to move forward. Whenever I felt myself getting upset, I would grab my phone and set the timer. It became automatic, and the results were promising. I noticed that, although I would usually still feel upset for longer than five minutes, the time it took me to accept whatever happened and get to a place of being at peace with it was happening faster and faster.

Then, something extraordinary happened. Two weeks after I began using the 5 Minute Rule, I faced the most significant setback in my budding sales career. It happened on a Sunday night. I had woken up that morning determined to reach my goal for the week. Orders were due the next morning, and I was $2,000 short of where I needed to be. Selling $1,000 in a day was significant, so selling the $2,000 I needed—on a Sunday—was unlikely. However, I was able to schedule two appointments for that afternoon, and although the first person didn't buy anything, the second one placed an order for over $2,300 and put me over my goal for the week! I called Jesse and excitedly shared the news. He told me that not only did I reach my goal but this order moved me into being the number one sales rep for the week. I was elated!

I spent the next hour imagining what it was going to be like when Jesse recognized me at our Wednesday night team meeting as the top sales rep for the week. I thought about how I was going to spend the money that I earned from my commission. Then, around 9 PM, my phone rang. It was the woman who placed the huge order. She explained that her husband was upset when he found out she spent so much money on knives, and she needed to cancel her order. My heart sank. I pleaded, reminding her of the 15-day trial and how much she loved the knives, but her mind was made up. *No . . . how could this happen?!* A few hours earlier, I was celebrating my largest order, having reached my goal and being the number one rep for the week, and now that was all gone, as was the commission I had already spent in my mind. Feeling extremely disappointed, I ended the phone call and instinctively set my timer for five minutes.

As the seconds began counting down, I naturally began resisting reality. *I can't believe she canceled. Stupid husband. If only he had been there to see the presentation, he probably would have loved Cutco as much as she did! This sucks. I wish that didn't happen… but it did. And I can't change it. So, what am I going to do now? I guess the only logical choice I really have is to stop resisting reality, accept that she canceled and that I didn't reach my goal for the week, and focus only on what I can control—waking up tomorrow morning and making calls to schedule more appointments.*

I took a deep breath and, on the exhale, said aloud, "Can't change it." I felt my tension subside, which prompted me to pick up my cell phone and look at my five-minute timer. Four minutes and thirty-two seconds remained. I thought, *What's the point in staying upset for the next four and a half minutes when I can just choose to accept my reality and be at peace with what I can't change, now, so that I can move on?* I turned my timer off, breathed a sigh of relief, and felt a surge of energy as I realized that I was now in control of my inner state. It felt like a superpower, to think that I now had the ability to accept anything that happened in my life, stop resisting it, and immediately be at peace.

No matter what happened, I could either resist reality and cause myself to be upset, or I could accept reality and be completely at peace with whatever happened. The choice was obvious. After only a few weeks of implementing the 5 Minute Rule, I went from thinking that five minutes wasn't enough time to realizing it wasn't necessary to stay upset for that long.

Looking back, I now see that my consciousness was elevated the moment I became aware that the fundamental cause of emotional pain is resisting reality and that we all have the power to let go of resistance and replace it with acceptance. Doing this enables us to stop creating emotional turmoil by resisting reality and wishing we could change things that are out of our control. Whether it happened five minutes ago or five decades ago, we can't go back and change the past. We can only choose whether we allow it to upset us or accept it and move on.

The objective of the 5 Minute Rule is to give yourself space to feel your emotions and then get to the point of acceptance. The end goal is to get to the point where you stop resisting reality and accept life as it is. You can do that by using the "Can't Change It" mantra as a reminder that if you can't change something, the most effective choice you have is to accept it and allow yourself to be at peace with whatever you can't change. Combining these two tools gives you an extremely powerful way to allow yourself the space to experience all your emotions without dwelling on things you simply cannot change for an extended period of time. To be clear, this only applies to things we truly cannot change (such as the past, other people, or global issues that are out of our immediate control). As the serenity prayer says, "God, grant me the serenity to accept the things I cannot change, the courage to change the things I can, and the wisdom to know the difference."

Accepting life as it is doesn't mean resigning yourself and giving up on making life better. Quite the contrary. When we are upset over something, our thinking is not clear, so we are not in an optimal state to make effective choices. However, when we are at peace, our thinking is clear, and we can both choose our optimal state of consciousness *and* make level-headed decisions that lead to proactive behaviors. When you constantly accept life exactly as it is, you are free to focus your energy on changing the things that are within your control. The faster you can get to the point where you say "Can't change it" and mean it, the faster you will achieve Inner Freedom.

Acceptance is the key that unlocks the door to Inner Freedom, and these three words, "Can't Change It," are like a key that unlocks the emotional handcuffs we constantly place on ourselves by self-creating and perpetuating emotional pain as a result of resisting reality. And whether it takes you five minutes or five months to get to the point where you consciously choose to say them, the moment you do is the moment you stop resisting reality and give yourself the gift of being at peace with life exactly as it is.

I've taught the 5 Minute Rule and "Can't Change It" mantra for more than 20 years, and I've received pictures from dozens of people who found it so impactful that they actually got permanent "Can't Change It" tattoos to remind them that they never again have to experience unhealthy and unnecessary emotional pain, because they now understand that they always have the power to *accept* life exactly as it is and *allow* themselves the Inner Freedom to be at peace.

Step B: Be Grateful for Each Moment

If I were to ask you to tell me about the best moment of your life, how would you respond? I imagine you'd probably take a few moments to search your memory and attempt to recall an extraordinary occasion or accomplishment, such as the birth of your first child, your wedding day, the time you achieved a significant goal, or the moment that you experienced your first _____ (insert any once-in-a-lifetime experience). It would likely be a meaningful event that, combined with the positive emotions you felt during or after, would prompt you to identify it as your "best" moment, one in which you almost certainly felt deeply grateful for whatever you experienced. You might even feel a sense of sadness as you look back and think that the best moment of your life is behind you, and you may never get to experience that again.

But wait—what if the best moment of your life isn't dependent on external conditions or a one-time event? What if it's actually something you have the ability to consciously *choose* rather than something that happens *to* you? Could it be that the best moments of our lives are determined by the depth of presence and gratitude that we allow ourselves to experience in and for the moment at hand, and thus, *you* can choose to experience quite literally *any* moment as the best moment of your life?

Yesterday, I played whiffle ball with my 10-year-old son in our backyard. As we played, I felt an overwhelming sense of gratitude and thought to myself, *This is the best moment of my life*. And it was. This morning, as I did my Miracle Morning, I wrote down what I was grateful for and then spent 10 minutes meditating in a state of genuine, heartfelt gratitude. And I thought to myself, *This is the best moment of my life*. And it was.

The best moment of your life isn't a competition between other moments. The best moment of your life exists in isolation and can be repeated and experienced as often as you want. It's simply a matter of being fully present and deeply grateful for each moment, no matter what you are experiencing.

If acceptance is the key that unlocks the door to Inner Freedom, gratitude is the doorway to sustained happiness. You simply have to walk through it every day. Walking through it means spending time focusing on what you're grateful for and hardwiring it into your nervous system, ideally first thing in the morning, last thing before you fall asleep, and as many times in between as possible. When we focus on what we're grateful for, we feel good. We foster feelings of joy and happiness. You could even say that the amount of gratitude you allow yourself to consciously focus on and experience determines how you feel about your life. In practice, this can be done during your Scribing time by writing down what you're grateful for, and during your period of purposeful Silence by using Emotional Optimization Meditation to deeply feel and hardwire gratitude so that it becomes one of your default states of consciousness.

Consider the ratio of time you spend complaining versus feeling grateful. Seriously, stop reading for a moment and consider the ratio. How much of your day is spent feeling deep, heartfelt gratitude for each moment, each life-giving breath, your loved ones, your safety, the roof over your head, the comfortable bed you get to sleep in, the food that gives you energy and enables you to sustain life? Versus how much of your day is spent feeling upset or complaining about things you don't like, people you don't like, or what you're worried about happening in the future? Consider that gratitude and complaining cannot coexist simultaneously; you must choose the one that best serves you in any moment.

By using the 5 Minute Rule and "Can't Change It" mantra to accept life exactly as it is, you're able to foster a state of Inner Freedom, which allows you the space to choose the next state of consciousness that best serves you. Gratitude exists as both an emotion and a state of consciousness. It is the emotion we feel when we appreciate *something*. It is the state of consciousness we embody when we appreciate *everything*.

Is it possible to be genuinely grateful for (literally) *everything*?

Every moment . . . even the painful ones?

Every experience . . . even the difficult ones?

Every adversity. . . even the unfair ones?

In a recent interview, Michael J. Fox was sharing how difficult and nearly unbearable it has become to live with his ever-worsening Parkinson's disease. "I recognize how hard this is for people, and I recognize how hard it is for me. But I have a certain set of skills that allow me to deal with this stuff, and I realize that with gratitude, optimism is sustainable. If you can find something to be grateful for, then you can find something to look forward to, and you carry on."

It is often the most difficult or painful times in our life that provide us with the greatest opportunities to learn, grow, and evolve.

It is also often said that hindsight is 20/20, and most of us have had the experience of looking back at difficult times in our lives and feeling grateful for the lessons learned or the growth we experienced. So, with that awareness, why allow ourselves to suffer in the present and delay seeing the benefits that we will gain from the challenges we face? Why not be grateful for every moment as we're experiencing it?

While gratitude (little *g*) can be a momentary "feeling" we have, usually due to some positive event or aspect of our lives, it becomes transformative when Gratitude (big *G*) becomes our state of consciousness—the lens through which we choose to experience each moment of our lives. I realized how crucial this distinction is when I faced another unimaginable life crisis.

At 37, I woke up in the middle of the night, struggling to breathe. My left lung had filled with fluid, and my heart and kidneys were failing. After many visits to different hospitals, late nights in the ER, having my lung drained seven times, and a lot of confusion from doctors, I finally made my way to MD Anderson Cancer Center, where I was diagnosed with an exceptionally rare and extremely aggressive form of cancer—acute lymphoblastic leukemia. Given a 20–30 percent survival rate, my odds of living more than a few weeks were grim. I had a wife, a seven-year-old daughter, and a four-year-old son at home, and being told that I had a 70–80 percent chance of dying was both terrifying and heartbreaking.

I dug deep and went back to the life lessons I had learned and used to overcome previous adversities. I told Ursula that I had decided there was a 100 percent chance that I would be among the 20–30 percent of those who beat this cancer, and I would maintain unwavering faith in that outcome every step of the way. I committed myself to fully accepting life exactly as it was and making peace with it, so that I could create the needed space to be genuinely grateful and maintain a positive and proactive mindset.

At the same time, I refused to complain or feel sorry for myself, and I made the conscious choice to be the *most* grateful I had ever been. I realized that I could choose to be genuinely grateful for each moment—including the difficult and painful ones. There is actual footage of this taking place, a scene in the *Miracle Morning* documentary where you see me uncontrollably bawling my eyes out. I had been in excruciating pain for 11 consecutive days after a nurse accidentally injected chemo into a nerve in my spine, which caused non-stop migraines. Despite being in unbearable pain, I say to the camera, "How hard this has been doesn't change my overall outlook, which is that I'm grateful for all of this, because the more difficult life is, the greater the opportunity for us to learn, to grow, to become better than we've ever been before, and then go out and make a difference for others with what we've learned and who we've become." When we consciously choose to be grateful in the midst of adversity, the adversity loses its power over us.

After enduring one of the most difficult time periods in my life, withstanding more than 650 hours of highly toxic and equally life-saving chemotherapy, combined with countless holistic protocols, I am grateful to say that I am now in remission and on a lifelong journey to remain healthy and free from cancer. In the end, despite the incredible hardships, the experience proved to be my greatest opportunity for growth—as a father, a husband, and a human being. And among the many invaluable lessons it taught me, one stands out:

Gratitude liberates us from suffering.

So, while focusing on what we're grateful for in each moment fosters positive mental and emotional states, it is when we're struggling and life is difficult that being in a state of Gratitude is even more consequential to our mental and emotional well-being. Gratitude is a universal lens through which we can interpret and experience *every* moment of our lives, including the most difficult, unpleasant, and painful ones.

Step C: Choose Your Optimal State of Consciousness

While emotional states are fleeting, states of consciousness are deeply rooted, ongoing, and present regardless of our changes in emotion. For example, Peace (often referred to as *inner peace*) is a state of consciousness. If you've elevated and conditioned your consciousness to live in a state of Peace, and a disturbing event upsets you, your state of consciousness doesn't change. You may still experience challenging emotions, such as frustration, anger, or sadness, but they will be short-lived, as you're able to quickly return to a state of Peace even amid tragedy, adversity, and uncertainty.

Similarly, if you've conditioned Gratitude as one of your default states of consciousness, then even when you're facing difficult times in your life, you will naturally feel grateful for all that you have. On the other hand, if the state of consciousness you're embodying is Fear, then you'll experience any disturbing event while in a fearful state, thereby amplifying the inner turmoil that the event causes you. We naturally resist things we are afraid of. Remember that our resistance to reality is the source of our emotional pain and instability.

After basking in feelings of gratitude, you are free to choose how you want to experience this next moment. You may want to feel love, joy, peace, playfulness, confidence, or possibly even sadness if you feel that you need to grieve, or anger, if you feel you need to process something that upset you. The fundamental distinction is that you are consciously and thoughtfully *choosing* your optimal state rather than allowing outside forces to determine it for you.

Obviously, you won't be perfect at embodying the Miracle Life immediately, but the goal isn't to be perfect; it's to make progress. Just like exercising in pursuit of your optimal physical state, it might take you months of daily practice before you get to where you want to be. By implementing your Miracle Mornings each day and incorporating the ABCs of the Miracle Life, you will develop the ability to choose your optimal state and enjoy spending each day in happiness and gratitude or whichever states you choose. I find it helpful to think of it like an ongoing game, where I get to choose my "prizes" (the elevated states of consciousness), and then I get to play the game every day to inch closer to the prizes.

Some days I feel like I'm "winning" when I successfully embody optimal states of consciousness and can effectively navigate adversity with grace and ease. Having practiced these tools for many years, I'm able to experience most of the day feeling at peace with anything that's out of my control and genuinely grateful for each moment, despite any challenges that might arise.

On the days, or in those moments, when I struggle—when I fall back to lower levels of consciousness and experience mental and emotional turmoil—I simply see it as losing a round of the game, and the next day I wake up and start fresh to play a new round.

When you see elevating your consciousness as a game, you will certainly struggle at times, especially when you're first learning how to play, but you can't fail. Even if you lose rounds, as long as you keep playing, you will continuously learn, grow, and become better each time you play.

Through daily repetition, you'll condition your optimal states of consciousness so that they become your default states of consciousness. The ultimate objective is to condition yourself to experience profound, all-encompassing states of inner peace, love, and gratitude, as well as unshakable confidence, motivation, and focus during each moment of your life.

I encourage you to use your Miracle Mornings to practice embodying the Miracle Life. As a Miracle Morning practitioner, you already have the framework (S.A.V.E.R.S.) to elevate your consciousness, so that you can be at peace with life exactly as it is, be genuinely grateful for each moment that you are alive, and consciously choose your optimal state of consciousness each day. And while all six of the S.A.V.E.R.S. can each uniquely serve as practices for integrating the Miracle Life (such as meditating while in an optimal state of consciousness or Scribing in your journal about what you want to accept and be at peace with), I want to keep this simple for you and focus on the one practice that I believe is most effective: *affirmations*.

I've created a relatively short (one printed page) set of affirmations that encapsulate the key lessons from this chapter so that you can remember and recite them daily and begin living your Miracle Life. You can also download and print the Miracle Life affirmations at MiracleMorning.com/resources.

The Miracle Life Affirmations

I am committed to elevating and conditioning my consciousness to a state of Inner Freedom so that I can choose how I experience each moment of my life. I've been blessed with one life, and I deserve to be genuinely at peace and happy. To do this, I will maintain the ABCs of the Miracle Life:

A: Accept Life Exactly As It Is

Now that I'm aware that emotional pain (aka inner turmoil) is self-created and perpetuated by my resistance to reality—focusing on things that are out of my control and wishing reality were different from what it is—I will accept life exactly as it is and choose to be at peace with all things that are out of my control. While I can't always control what happens in my life, I am always free to choose how I experience each moment of my life.

To help me overcome my unconscious resistance and accept life exactly as it is, I will apply the 5 Minute Rule (setting a timer and giving myself five minutes to feel whatever emotions naturally arise within me). Then, when the timer goes off, I will simply say, "Can't change it" to acknowledge and remind myself that, since I can't go back in time and change whatever happened, my only logical choice is to accept and be at peace with what I can't change so that I can experience Inner Freedom. Remember, acceptance is the key that unlocks the door to Inner Freedom.

Last, I will remember that being at peace with something doesn't necessarily mean I'm happy about it. But thankfully, peace is a state of consciousness that is far more powerful and sustainable than any short-lived emotion. Peace is emotionally neutral, and from that state, I can choose to be happy, grateful, or any other state that serves me.

B: Be Grateful for Each Moment

Once I've chosen to accept reality exactly as it is, thereby allowing myself to experience the peace that is always available in a state of Inner Freedom, I am committed to moving beyond mere acceptance by choosing to be genuinely grateful for each moment.

I understand that gratitude is the lens through which I can choose to experience and enjoy every moment of my life—including the difficult ones. Even when I am enduring difficult times, I can choose to be grateful for the lessons and growth that will result from facing and overcoming my adversity with a positive mindset, enabling me to become a better, more capable version of myself.

I recognize that every moment exists in a state of inherent perfection, and I get to choose how I experience each moment. I realize that my life is the present moment, so I choose to allow myself to feel genuine, heartfelt gratitude for each moment. Remember, gratitude is the doorway to happiness.

C: Choose My Optimal State of Consciousness

While emotions are often spontaneous and short-lived, states of consciousness are underlying ways of experiencing life. Dwelling on negative states such as guilt, shame, fear, or anger causes me to suffer unnecessarily and miss out on states like love, happiness, peace, gratitude, and joy.

The default state I choose is *Inner Freedom* because it enables me to be at peace with what I can't change so that I can choose how I experience each moment that I am alive. No matter what happens, even when my circumstances are difficult or painful, I choose to be at peace and grateful so that I can enjoy this one life I've been blessed to live. This is my Miracle Life.

Elevating your consciousness is not a one-time event. It is an ongoing process that is accomplished through consistent conditioning, like increasing your physical strength is accomplished through consistent exercise. I highly encourage you to begin by reading these affirmations every day for the remainder of your 30-day Journey, then continue for as long as it takes to condition your consciousness so that Inner Freedom becomes your default state.

While you can read/recite these affirmations during your Miracle Morning to help you start your day in an optimal state of consciousness, you might also find it beneficial to reread them during your Miracle Evening to remind yourself that you have the ability to accept life exactly as it is, be grateful for each moment, and choose your optimal state of consciousness as you prepare to fall asleep.

I'd also like to leave you with a handful of my favorite books that I've found to be the most helpful when it comes to continuing to learn how to elevate our consciousness, so that you can add them to your reading list. Here are a few of my favorites (which I initially read during my Miracle Morning and continue to reread my underlined text at night, before bed, to help me feel peaceful as I fall asleep):

- *The Untethered Soul* and *Living Untethered* by Michael Singer
- *Loving What Is* by Byron Katie
- *Peace Is Every Step* by Thich Nhat Hanh
- *The Inner Work* by Mathew Micheletti and Ashley Cottrell
- *Awareness* by Anthony De Mello

Final Thoughts on the Miracle Life

The Miracle Life is available to all of us but is only lived by those who are willing to accept life exactly as it is, be grateful in each moment, and consciously choose their optimal state of consciousness.

I know firsthand how difficult and painful circumstances can be. I also know that we can choose how we interpret and experience each moment. We can be at peace and even be the happiest and most grateful we have ever been—*while* we endure the most difficult time in our life. If we do not allow ourselves to experience peace and gratitude now, what makes us think the future will be any different?

No matter what life throws at you, you can choose how you experience every moment that you are alive. You can choose to be at peace. You choose to be grateful. You can choose to be happy. You can choose to enjoy every moment of this one life you've been blessed to live. You can choose to live the Miracle Life.

CONCLUSION

Let Today Be the Day You Give Up Who You've Been for Who You Can Become

"Every day, think as you wake up, 'Today I am fortunate to have woken up, I am alive, I have a precious human life, I am not going to waste it. I am going to use all my energies to develop myself, to expand my heart out to others. I am going to benefit others as much as I can.'"

—Dalai Lama

"Things do not change. We change."

—Henry David Thoreau

Where you are is a result of who you *were*, but where you end up depends entirely on who you choose to be from this moment forward.

This is your time. Don't put off creating and experiencing the life—happiness, health, wealth, success, and love—that you truly want and deserve for another day. As my mentor Kevin Bracy always urged: "Don't wait to be great." If you want your life to improve, you have to improve yourself first. Stay committed to completing your Miracle Morning 30-Day Journey so that you can continue becoming the person you need to be to create everything you want for your life and help others do the same.

We Are Elevating the Consciousness of Humanity Together

When I first began practicing the Miracle Morning, it was a selfish pursuit. I was struggling financially and needed a solution. I wasn't thinking about anybody else.

However, over the years, and especially since becoming a parent, I've realized that doing the Miracle Morning is as much about how it enables me to show up for others as it is about how it enables me to show up for myself.

Beginning each day with the S.A.V.E.R.S. helps me to be a better father, a better husband, and a better all-around human being. It enables me to be more patient, loving, and intentional in everything I do. For example, I have affirmations for each of my most important relationships, including my "Super Awesome Fun Dad" affirmations that remind me how I'm committed to showing up for my kids. I also read my "Husband of Ursula's Dreams" affirmations each day, which articulate and remind me of how I'm committed to showing up for my wife. I have similar affirmations to help me optimize how I show up for all people.

So, as you begin your Miracle Morning journey and integrate the S.A.V.E.R.S. into your daily life, I encourage you to keep this in mind. Consider how you can incorporate those you love, and those you lead, into your Miracle Mornings. Consider the impact that becoming the best version of yourself will have on others. On a grander scale, consider the impact of millions of us around the world doing the same.

Remember, the Miracle Morning Mission is to elevate the consciousness of humanity, one morning (and one person) at a time. Every morning, you are that one person. By elevating your own consciousness—becoming more aware and intentional about how your thoughts, words, and actions impact you and others—you are quite literally elevating the consciousness of humanity.

Thank you so much for caring enough about yourself and others to wake up each day and dedicate time to fulfilling your potential.

With love and gratitude,

Hal

A SPECIAL INVITATION

(In Case You Missed It the First Time)

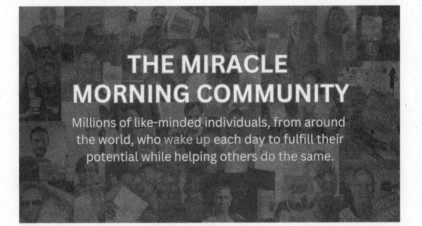

THE MIRACLE MORNING COMMUNITY

Millions of like-minded individuals, from around the world, who wake up each day to fulfill their potential while helping others do the same.

If you'd like to connect with and get support from other like-minded Miracle Morning practitioners as you read this book, whether to ask questions or just observe and learn from how they're approaching their practice, I invite you to join the **Miracle Morning Community**.

What began as a Facebook group with me, my parents, and five of my friends has grown into an online community with over 300,000 members from more than one hundred countries. It's always free to join, and while you'll find many people who are just beginning their Miracle Morning journey, you'll also find those who have been practicing for years and who will happily share advice, support, and guidance to help you accelerate your success.

As the author of *The Miracle Morning*, I wanted to create a space where we can all come together to connect, ask questions, share best practices, support one another, discuss the book, post videos, find an accountability partner, and even swap smoothie recipes and exercise routines. I never imagined that the Miracle Morning Community would become one of the most positive, engaged, and supportive online communities in the world, but it truly has!

You can begin connecting with other Miracle Morning practitioners. Just visit MiracleMorningCommunity.com and request to join. I check in regularly (almost every single day), posting content and engaging in the comments, so I look forward to seeing you there!

Miracle Morning Community Resources: The App and the Movie

There are two additional resources (both of which are free) that can help you as you begin your Miracle Morning journey: the Miracle Morning Routine app and *The Miracle Morning* movie.

The single most requested resource by members of the Miracle Morning Community has been a mobile app to track your Miracle Mornings and help you become consistent and accountable. Additional features include a built-in journal with writing prompts, an affirmations creator, customizable timers, and optional guided audio tracks to lead you through the S.A.V.E.R.S. (silence, affirmations, visualization, exercise, reading, and scribing) so that you can complete your Miracle Morning by simply clicking "play" and following along. The app is available for both iPhone and Android at **MiracleMorning.com/app**.

Filmed over the course of six years, *The Miracle Morning* movie is an inspiring feature-length documentary that goes beyond the book and actually shows you how people are transforming their lives, one morning at a time. It also takes you into the homes of world-renowned authors, doctors, scientists, entrepreneurs, and professional athletes to reveal how these highly productive individuals start their day. It also takes you into one of the most difficult times of my life. Two years into filming, I was unexpectedly diagnosed with a rare form of cancer and given a 30 percent chance of surviving. Our director kept the cameras rolling in order to capture my mindset and the holistic approach I used to beat cancer in hopes that it might inspire someone else who is battling cancer or some other disease. You can watch the extended trailer and access the full film at **MiracleMorning.com/movie**.

So far, the app has a rating of 4.9 out of 5.0 stars and the movie has a rating of 4.6 out of 5.0 stars, so I hope these free resources are as helpful for you as they've been for others!

Welcome to the Miracle Morning Community!

GET THE MIRACLE MORNING APP!

Your Morning Routine Companion

The Miracle Morning app is a resource that supports you in implementing everything you learn in the book.

Download the app at MiracleMorning.com/App

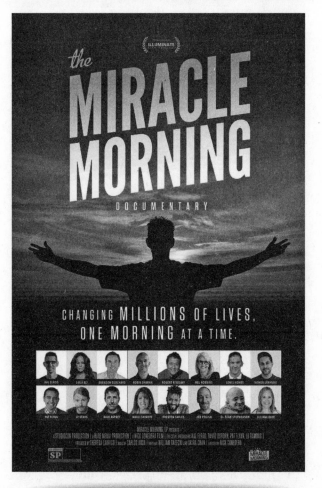

ACKNOWLEDGMENTS

B e sure to at least read the last two paragraphs (they're to *you*). This may be the most challenging part of writing a book. Not because I am short on people to acknowledge, quite the opposite. There are so many people who have made a significant impact in my life and on this book that I think it may be impossible to thank them all in the next few pages. In fact, doing so could probably take up an entire book itself. The sequel to this book could be titled *The Miracle Morning: Acknowledgments*. I don't know that too many people would buy it, but I would definitely enjoy writing it. ☺

First, I want to give a heartfelt thanks to the extraordinary woman who carried me around for 9.5 months and gifted me with the miracle of life—my mother, Julie Wilson. Mom, I love you so much! Thank you for always believing in me and disciplining me when I needed it. (Okay, I still need it.) Oh, and *you* need to come to visit more often!

To my father, Mark Elrod. Dad, of all my best friends, you are my *best* friend. I am the man I am today because of the father you have been for me my entire life. You have instilled so many values and qualities in me, which I am even more grateful for now that I know I will be passing them on to my children. I love you, Dad.

To Hayley, you're the best sister ever. Hands down. No competition. However, you are not only a great sister but also one of my best friends. You are authentic, supportive, kind, and you're *almost* as funny as I am! Seriously, I am so grateful that *you* are my sister—I couldn't imagine a better one.

To my baby sister and our angel, Amery, watching over us from heaven. I miss you, Sis. Thank you for watching over all of us.

To my wife-for-life, Ursula. I still marvel at how perfect you are for me, and I couldn't be more grateful to create and share our lives together. And how 'bout them cute kids we made, huh? Thank you for blessing me with Sophia and Halsten. With you at the helm, I know our family is destined for a lifetime of love and happiness.

To my daughter, Sophia (aka Sophinator). I love you so much!!! You are everything I ever hoped for in a daughter, and I couldn't be more grateful for the joy and happiness that you bring to my life every day. You are kind, brilliant, creative, and so funny! And I'm so grateful that I am blessed to be your dad!

To my son, Halsten (aka Halstino), you are the kindest, most loving, and most generous human being I have ever met. Since you were two years old and able to talk, you've always looked out for the best interest of other people. I've always said that you seemed to have been born already exemplifying the values that I've worked a lifetime to learn. I love you so much, son!

To my aunts, uncles, cousins, and grandparents, I am so thankful for the immeasurable amount of love that you have always shown me. Some of my greatest memories are spending time with you. I love you all so much!

To my in-laws—Marek, Maryla, Steve, Linda, Adam, and Ania—I am grateful to be a part of your family.

To Tiffany Hammond, Chief Operations Officer of The Miracle Morning. You are family. You are also one of the kindest and most loyal, selfless, resilient, and hard-working human beings I have ever met. Who could have ever guessed that a chance encounter at Yard

House would turn into a near decade of working together?! Thank you for all you contribute to my life, my family's life, and our collective Miracle Morning Mission. You've shown up for me in ways that no one else has. I love you so much, Tiff!

To Brianna Greenspan, the O.G. MMer! You are an angel to me. You have not only been the most dedicated advocate and supporter of the Miracle Morning since the beginning, but you have been one of my best friends as well. From being on those Miracle Morning "Movement Maker" calls way back in 2012 to supporting me through my cancer journey, showing up for my family, and giving me brilliant advice when I need it (and we both know that I often need it), you are one of the most important people in my life. Most recently, you've dedicated yourself to developing *The Miracle Morning in Schools* program and are making a profound impact in the lives of educators and youth in ways I only dreamt of. Words can't describe how much I love and appreciate you, Bri!

To Honorée Corder (also known as "the book whisperer"), I truly can't thank you enough for all of your help throughout the years! You've been instrumental in helping me to bring the Miracle Morning to countless people through the book series, and I feel so fortunate that our paths crossed. You are truly one of the best in the world at teaching people how to write, publish, and monetize their books! And while you've contributed so much to the Miracle Morning Mission, what I am personally most thankful for is how you stepped up to help me after I was diagnosed with cancer. Thank you so much for your love, support, and friendship, Honorée. I love you, and I am eternally grateful to you!

To Josh Eidenberg, thank you for pouring so much of yourself into the Miracle Morning Mission and constantly thinking of ways we can better serve the Miracle Morning Community. Thank you for relentlessly encouraging me to allow you to finally create the long-overdue Miracle Morning app, which is now helping tens of thousands of people to elevate their consciousness every single day. Josh, you are as brilliant and creative as you are kind and generous, and I feel deeply grateful and privileged to be able to work alongside you to elevate human consciousness.

To Stephanie Blackbird, your years of unwavering commitment to supporting and moderating the Miracle Morning Community have been nothing short of extraordinary. You are fiercely loyal and have always gone over and above to serve. Thank you so much. I love you, Steph!

To Veronica Vielma and Zach Eichler, your contributions to the Miracle Morning Mission have been invaluable. We are impacting more people than ever thanks to your efforts. I can't thank you enough for how you show up for our team and our community.

To Celeste Fine. I don't know if you're an angel or a genie or what, but you've continuously created miracles in my life. On more than one occasion, I've written down a goal or a dream that was so big I had no idea how I would accomplish it. Then, suddenly, you showed up with the means to make my dreams come true. And you do it from a place of love, truly looking out for my best interest. I appreciate you so much, Celeste!

To Scott Hoffman, thank you for believing in The Miracle Morning and in me. Together, I have unwavering faith that we are going to positively impact many more lives.

To Glenn Yeffeth, CEO of BenBella and my chief editor for this book. Working alongside you to update this manuscript has been such a pleasure, and this book turned out so much better than I could have ever imagined, thanks to you.

To each of *The Miracle Morning* co-authors, thank you for contributing your love and wisdom to the book series! Let's keep helping as many people as we can.

To Emily Klein, Elizabeth Pratt, Elaine Pofeldt, and Julie Strauss—my brilliant editing team—thank you for helping me to communicate my ideas in a way that will surely resonate deeply with readers. This book reads so much more clearly because of you, contributing your unique talents and perspectives.

To Dino Marino, ever since Honorée introduced us, you have been extraordinarily kind and supportive, using your talents with graphic design to make the Miracle Morning more eye-catching so that more people get to experience the benefits. Your contributions are invaluable and immeasurable.

To my closest friends—my *circle of influence*—any person would be lucky to have any one of you in his life, and I somehow ended up with *all* of you! We've shared *a lot* of great times together, but beyond that, it is *who you are* that makes me strive to be better. If it is true that we are the average of the five people we spend the most time with, I've got nothing to worry about! For your lifelong friendship, I love you Jeremy Katen, Matt Recore, Jon Vroman, Jon Berghoff, Jesse Levine, Brad Weimert, Jeremy "Brotha James" Reisig, John Ruhlin, Justin Donald, David Osborn, and Mike McCarthy—and to my many friends that I may not have mentioned here, know that it's not because I don't love you. I do. I just forgot about you while I was writing this.

To my extended family at Cutco and Vector, I can't thank you enough for the incredible contributions you have made to my life. So much of who I am today and what I wrote in this book wouldn't be possible without the opportunity you provided me.

To my brilliant friend and the creator of BookMama.com, Linda Sivertsen—you are so talented and have such a gift for making any author's book idea into a bestselling masterpiece. Thank you for contributing your gifts to this book.

To Kevin Bracy, I was sitting in your seminar just days before my first Miracle Morning, and your words were the catalyst for me to overcome my limiting belief that I was *not* a morning person. Just when I was about to give up, your words of wisdom reminded me that, "If you want your life to be different, you have to be willing to do something different, first." I may have never attempted to wake up at 5 AM—let alone written this book—if it wasn't for you.

To James Malinchak, when I shared *The Miracle Morning* with you for the first time, you were genuinely excited, and you expanded my vision of what was possible: "Hal, I don't think you even see how big this is going to be, and how many people this is going to impact!" You have personally inspired me and tens of thousands of authors, speakers, and coaches to believe in our message, see it bigger, and impact more people. You did that for me, and I can't thank you enough!

To J. Brad Britton, you taught me one of the most valuable lessons, which I continue to live my life by and share with anyone who will listen—*do the right thing, not the easy thing*. You don't just teach it; you live it. Thank you for always bringing out the best in others like you did for me.

To everyone who supported the original launch of this book back in 2012, your selflessness and commitment to paying forward the benefits you've received from the Miracle Morning have left me speechless. First, I have to thank the Miracle Morning Launch Team—what a blast it was working with you to promote this book. I will forever be grateful and indebted to you. Special thanks to Kyle Smith, Isaac Stegman, Geri Azinger, Marc Ensign, Colleen Elliot Linder, Dashama, Mark Hartley, Dave Powders, Jon Berghoff, Jon Vroman, Jeremy Katen, Ryan Whiten, Brianna Greenspan, Robert Gonzalez, Carey Smolenski, Ryan Casey, Peter Voogd, and Greg Strine.

Finally, to you and every member of our collective human family, I believe that we all have infinitely more in common than the perceived differences that far too many people cling to. As a part of my family, I love and appreciate you more than you know.

All right, now it's time to stop reading and start creating. Never settle. Create the life you deserve to live, and help others do the same.

REFERENCES

Chapter 1

Collins, Nick. "Early Risers Get Ahead of the Game." *Telegraph*. September 15, 2011. Available online at: www.telegraph.co.uk/news/health/news/8763618/Early-risers-get-ahead-of-the-game.html

El Issa, Erin. "2017 American Household Credit Card Debt Survey." *Nerd Wallet*. Available online at: www.nerdwallet.com/blog/average-credit-card-debt-household

Lubin, Gus, and Gillett, Rachel. "21 Successful People Who Wake Up Incredibly Early." *Business Insider*. April 27, 2016. Available online at: www.businessinsider.com/successful-people-who-wake-up-really-early-2016-4#twitter-and-square-ceo-jack-dorsey-wakes-up-before-dawn-

Randler, Christopher. "Proactive People Are Morning People." *Journal of Applied Social Psychology* 39, no. 12 (December 9, 2009): 2787–2797. Available online at: onlinelibrary.wiley.com/doi/10.1111/j.1559-1816.2009.00549.x/abstract

Rauh, Sherry. "Is Fat the New Normal?" *WebMD*. June 2010. Available online at: www.webmd.com/diet/obesity/features/is-fat-the-new-normal#1

Smith, Michael. "APSS: Early Risers Tend to Score Higher Grades." *MedPage Today*. June 10, 2008. Available online at: www.medpage today.com/meetingcoverage/apss/9772

"State of the Global Workplace." Gallup. (2017). Available online at: news.gallup.com/reports/220313/state-global-workplace-2017 .aspx#formheader

"Survey Finds Nearly Three-Quarters (72%) of Americans Feel Lonely." American Osteopathic Association press release. October 2016. Available online at: www.prnewswire.com/news-releases/survey -finds-nearly-three-quarters-72-of-americans-feel-lonely-30034 2742.html

Whiteman, Honor. "Poor Sleep Habits Increase Weight Gain for Adults with Genetic Obesity Risk." *MedicalNewsToday*. March 3, 2017. Available online at: www.medicalnewstoday.com /articles/316186.php

Chapter 2

"Americans Are Tired Most of the Week." YouGov. Available online at: www.statista.com/chart/3534/americans-are-tired-most-of-the-week

"Cancer Facts and Figures 2017." American Cancer Society. Available online at: www.cancer.org/content/dam/cancer-org/research/cancer -facts-and-statistics/annual-cancer-facts-and-figures/2017/cancer -facts-and-figures-2017.pdf

Carr, Theresa. "Too Many Meds? America's Love Affair with Prescription Medication." *Consumer Reports*. August 3, 2017. Available online at: www.consumerreports.org/prescription-drugs/too-many-meds -americas-love-affair-with-prescription-medication/#nation

Jacoby, Sarah. "Here's What the Divorce Rate Actually Means." *Refinery29*. February 2, 2017. Available online at: www.refinery29 .com/2017/01/137440/divorce-rate-in-america-statistics

LaMagna, Maria. "Americans Now Have the Highest Credit Card Debt in U.S. History." *MarketWatch*. August 8, 2017. Available

online at https://www.marketwatch.com/story/us-households
-will-soon-have-as-much-debt-as-they-had-in-2008-2017-04-03

"Median Age of the Resident Population of the United States from 1960 to 2016." Statista. Available online at: www.statista.com /statistics/241494/median-age-of-the-us-population

"Report: How Satisfied Are U.S. Workers with Their Salaries?" *Indeed* (blog). January 25, 2018. Available online at: blog.indeed.com /2018/01/25/salary-report

Chapter 3

Abrams, Abigail. "Divorce Rate in U.S. Drops to Nearly 40-Year Low." *Time*. December 5, 2016. Available online at: time.com/4575495 /divorce-rate-nearly-40-year-low

"Cancer Facts and Figures 2017." American Cancer Society. Available online at: www.cancer.org/content/dam/cancer-org/research/cancer -facts-and-statistics/annual-cancer-facts-and-figures/2017/cancer -facts-and-figures-2017.pdf

Elkins, Kathleen. "Here's How Much the Average American Family Has Saved for Retirement." CNBC. September 12, 2016. Available online at: www.cnbc.com/2016/09/12/heres-how-much-the-average-american -family-has-saved-for-retirement.html

Kantor, Elizabeth D., et al. "Trends in Prescription Drug Use among Adults in the United States from 1999–2012." *JAMA* 314, no. 17 (2015): 1818–1831. Available online at: pubmed.ncbi.nlm.nih.gov/26529160

Mitchell, Nia, et al. "Obesity: Overview of an Epidemic." *Psychiatric Clinics of North America* 34, no. 4 (2011): 717–732. Available online at: www .ncbi.nlm.nih.gov/pmc/articles/PMC3228640

Poushter, Jacob. "Worldwide, People Divided on Whether Life Today Is Better Than in the Past." Pew Research Center, Global Attitudes and Trends. December 5, 2017. Available online at: www .pewglobal.org/2017/12/05/worldwide-people-divided-on-whether -life-today-is-better-than-in-the-past

Chapter 4

Bucklan, Erinn. "Is the Snooze Button Bad for You?" CNN. February 7, 2014. Available online at: edition.cnn.com/2014/02/06/health/upwave -snooze-button

DiGuilio, Sarah. "How What You Eat Affects Sleep." NBCNews.com. October 19, 2017. Available online at: www.nbcnews.com/better /health/how-what-you-eat-affects-how-you-sleep-ncna805256

"Effect of Short Sleep Duration on Daily Activities—United States, 2005–2008." *Centers for Disease Control Weekly* 60, no. 8 (March 4, 2011): 239–242. Available online at: www.cdc.gov/mmwr/preview /mmwrhtml/mm6008a3.htm

Léger, Damien; Beck, François; Richard, Jean-Baptiste; Sauvet, Fabien; and Faraut, Brice. "The Risks of Sleeping 'Too Much': Survey of a National Representative Sample of 24671 Adults (INPES Health Barometer)." *Plos One* 9, no. 9 (2014): e106950. Available online at: journals.plos.org/plosone/article?id=10.1371/journal.pone.0106950

Chapter 5

Achten, J. and Jeukendrup, A. E. "Optimizing Fat Oxidation Through Exercise and Diet." *Nutrition* 20, no. 7–8 (Jul–Aug 2004): 716–727. Available online at: www.ncbi.nlm.nih.gov/pubmed/15212756

Marshall, Mallika. "The Big Benefits of Plain Water." *Harvard Health Blog*. May 26, 2016. Available online at: www.health.harvard.edu/blog /big-benefits-plain-water-201605269675

Chapter 6

Creswell, J. David; Dutcher, Janine M.; Klein, William M. P.; Harris, Peter R.; and Levine, John M. "Self-Affirmation Improves Problem-Solving under Stress." *Plos One* (May 1, 2013). Available online: journals.plos .org/plosone/article?id=10.1371/journal.pone.0062593

Ketler, Alanna. "Scientific Studies Show How Writing in a Journal Can Actually Benefit Your Emotional and Physical Well-Being." *Collective*

Evolution. January 23, 2017. Available online at: www.collective
-evolution.com/2017/01/23/scientific-studies-show-how-writing
-in-a-journal-can-actually-benefit-your-emotional-physical
-well-being

Lindsay, Emily K., and Creswell, J. David. "Helping the Self Help
Others: Self-Affirmation Increases Self-Compassion and Pro-Social
Behaviors." *Frontiers in Psychology* 5 (2014): 421. Available online at:
www.ncbi.nlm.nih.gov/pmc/articles/PMC4026714

"Meditation Benefits." American Meditation Society. Available online at:
americanmeditationsociety.org/meditation/benefits

Oppong, Thomas. "The Creative Brain on Silence (How Solitude
Inspires Creativity)." *Medium*. March 2, 2018. Available online
at: medium.com/@alltopstartups/the-creative-brain-on-silence
-how-solitude-inspires-creativity-145f7fec907f

Ranganathan, V. K.; Siemionow, V.; Liu, J. Z.; Sahgal, V.; and Yue, G. H.
"From Mental Power to Muscle Power: Gaining Strength by Using the
Mind." *Neuropsychologia* 42, no. 7 (2017): 944–956. Available online at:
www.ncbi.nlm.nih.gov/pubmed/14998709

Reynolds, Gretchen. "Yoga May Be Good for the Brain." *New York Times*.
June 1, 2016. Available online at: well.blogs.nytimes.com/2016/06/01
/yoga-may-be-good-for-the-brain

"Transcendental Meditation: Oprah and Other Celebs Who Embrace the
Practice." *Huffington Post*. March 26, 2012. Available online at: www
.huffingtonpost.com/2012/03/26/transcendental-meditation-oprah
-winfrey_n_1379001.html

Chapter 8

Chance, Zoe; Gorlin, Margarita; and Dhar, Ravi. "Why Choosing Healthy
Foods Is Hard, and How to Help: Presenting the 4Ps Framework for
Behavior Change." *Customer Needs and Solutions* 1 (September 12,
2014): 253–262. Available online at: link.springer.com/article/10.1007
/s40547-014-0025-9

"The Best Diet: Quality Counts." *Nutrition Source*. Harvard T. H. Chan
    School of Public Health. Available online at: www.hsph.harvard.edu
    /nutritionsource/healthy-weight/best-diet-quality-counts

Chapter 9

"How Long Does It Take for Something to Become a Habit?" *Examined
    Existence*. Available online at: examinedexistence.com/how-long
    -does-it-take-for-something-to-become-a-habit

ABOUT THE AUTHOR

Hal Elrod is a family man, first and foremost. He is a loyal husband to his wife of 14 years and a dedicated father to their two children.

He is also living proof that every single one of us has the ability to overcome any adversity, fulfill our potential, and create the life we want while helping others do the same.

At age 20, Hal was found dead at the scene after his car was hit head-on by a drunk driver at over 70 miles per hour. His heart stopped beating for six minutes, he broke 11 bones, suffered permanent brain damage, and was told by doctors that he would never walk again.

Then, at age 37, he nearly died a second time when his heart, lungs, and kidneys were failing, and he was diagnosed with a rare and extremely aggressive form of cancer (acute lymphoblastic leukemia). After being given a 20–30 percent chance of surviving, Hal once again defied seemingly insurmountable odds to beat cancer.

Having survived multiple near-death experiences and impacted millions of lives through his books and speeches, Hal is now on a mission to elevate the consciousness of humanity, one morning and one person at a time. As an international keynote speaker, host of the Achieve Your Goals podcast, executive producer of *The Miracle Morning* documentary, and author of more than a dozen books, which have been translated into 37 languages and sold over 3 million copies, he's doing exactly that.

Hal has also shared his story on *The Today Show*, been featured in SUCCESS Magazine, and written for Entrepreneur.com.

Visit **HalElrod.com** to learn more or book Hal to speak at your event.

The Miracle Morning Book Series

Find the following titles at MiracleMorning.com/books or Amazon.com.

Foreign Translations

Now Available in 37 languages, including ...

Spanish, French, Dutch, Italian, Japanese, simplified Chinese, traditional Chinese, Korean, Portuguese, Russian, German, Romanian, Taiwanese, Polish, Ukrainian, Vietnamese, Thai, Croatian, Arabic, Albanian, Czech, Mongolian, and Hebrew, with more languages being translated each year.